The Vegetable Finder

Sources for almost 3000 commercially available vegetable varieties

Published by the Henry Doubleday Research Association
Researching, demonstrating and promoting environmentally
friendly growing techniques

Edited by Jeremy Cherfas

Published by The Henry Doubleday Research Association
Ryton-on-Dunsmore, Coventry, CV8 3LG

Distributed by Moorland Publishing Co. Ltd
Moor Farm Road, Airfield Estate, Ashbourne, Derbyshire, DE6 1HD

© The Henry Doubleday Research Association 1993

ISBN 0-905343-18-2

Printed in Great Britain by The Cromwell Press Ltd
Broughton Gifford, Melksham, Wiltshire, SN12 8PH

Printed on environmentally friendly, acid-free paper from managed forests

Contents

Introduction

Would you buy a potato called "Pomme de Terre"? What would you think of a supplier who offered three different potatoes, one called "Spud," one called "Tattie" and one called "Pomme de Terre"?

These are not fanciful examples; they have exact equivalents in the wonderful world of oriental vegetables, where a Babel of names currently exists. Some people use the Japanese name for a Chinese vegetable, others are happy to quote two different Chinese dialect names for the same vegetable, and some cannot be fathomed at all.

I know this not because I am an expert but because Joy Larkcom is. She has done all the hard work for me, making sense of the huge variety of oriental vegetables coming onto the market. Her book, *Oriental Vegetables: The Complete Guide for Garden and Kitchen*, (published by John Murray) is an absolute delight, full of cultural details, mouthwatering recipes, and glimpses into the garden habits of some of the most efficient growers in the world. I have used it to go through the offerings of our own seed suppliers to see if I can bring some order to an otherwise extremely confused state of affairs.

The result is a table that shows the various synonyms under which seed suppliers offer oriental vegetables, which I have tried to relate to the names Joy Larkcom favours; I regard these as approved names, although I should stress that I have not been able to check them with the authority herself. The problem with this approach is that sometimes I have to guess at exactly what a seed supplier means by using a particular name. I am ready to admit that this may be a source of confusion, but I would hope that the table removes more confusion than it creates. So, if you are looking for a particular vegetable or variety in the main body of *The Vegetable Finder*, and cannot find it, then you may have more luck if you look in the table of oriental synonyms and see if it isn't perhaps lurking under another name.

Synonyms under which some oriental vegetables appear in seed suppliers' catalogues

Bayam *is another name for*	Amaranthus
Bok Choy	Headed Chinese Cabbage
Brocoletto	Choy Sum
Calaloo	Amaranthus
Celery Cabbage	Headed Chinese Cabbage
Celtuce	Lettuce Stem
Ceylon Spinach	Basella
Chinese Celery Cabbage	Pak Choi
Chinese Kale	Chinese Broccoli
Chinese Leaves	Headed Chinese Cabbage
Chinese Leek	Chinese Chives
Chinese Lettuce	Lettuce Stem
Chinese Mustard (Greens)	Mustard Greens
Chinese Spinach	Amaranthus
Chinese White Cabbage	Pak Choi
Chingensai	Pak Choi
Chop Suey Greens	Chrysanthemum Greens
Crosnes	Chinese Artichoke
Daikon	Radish
Edible Oil Seed Rape	Choy Sum
Flat Black Pak Choi	Rosette Pak Choi
Flat Pak Choi	Rosette Pak Choi
Flowering Pak Choi	Choy Sum
Flowering White Cabbage	Choy Sum
Gai Choy	Mustard Greens
Gai Lan	Chinese Broccoli
Garlic Chives	Chinese Chives
Gobo	Burdock
Green in Snow	Mustard Greens
Hon Tsai Tai	Choy Sum (Purple Flowered)
Hong Tsoi Sum	Choy Sum (Purple Flowered)
Indian Mustard (Greens)	Mustard Greens
Indian Spinach	Basella
Japanese Artichoke	Chinese Artichoke
Japanese Greens	Chrysanthemum Greens

Japanese Parsley	Mitsuba
Kaai Laan Tsoi	Chinese Broccoli
Kaai Tsoi	Mustard Greens
Kailan	Chinese Broccoli
Kosaitai	Choy Sum (Purple Flowered)
Leaf Mustard	Mustard Greens
Malabar Spinach	Basella
Michihili	Headed Chinese Cabbage
Mooli	Radish
Mustard Cabbage	Mustard Greens
Mustard Cabbage	Pak Choi
Mustard Spinach	Komatsuna
Pak Tsoi Sum	Choy Sum
Pe-tsai	Headed Chinese Cabbage
Purple Flowered Choy Sum	Choy Sum
Shungiku	Chrysanthemum Greens
Spinach Mustard	Komatsuna
Taisin	Pak Choi
Tasai	Rosette Pak Choi
Tatsoi	Rosette Pak Choi
White Flowering Broccoli	Chinese Broccoli
Wong Bok	Headed Chinese Cabbage

The confusion surrounding oriental vegetables may be stopping some people from trying these estimable edibles, because it would be easy to be paralysed by the apparently endless choice. The truth is, as Joy Larkcom points out, that we have barely begun to explore these vegetables and varieties. However, it will not be easy to do so until the seed suppliers get together and agree on some standard sorts of descriptions.

Just the job, in fact, for a National List! It may seem odd for me to advocate a National List, as we have always argued in the past that it is the National List that has made so many of our old beloved varieties unattainable today. In fact, it is not the National List as such, but the fact that the cost of keeping a variety on the list is a fixed fee. Naturally, the varieties favoured by gardeners cannot compete with those designed for the big professional growers, so it is the gardeners' varieties that vanish. The great benefit of a National List is that it ought to sort out the confusion of names that currently afflicts oriental vegetables. But unless the system is made much fairer it will continue to threaten the commercial existence of varieties that suit the small grower, and we will continue to press for a more equitable system.

This year has seen a slight change in the availability of varieties. Our latest figures suggest a slight increase in the number of open-pollinated varieties (1990 compared to 1973) and a slight decrease in F1 hybrids (822 compared to 829 last year). The increase in open-pollinated varieties is, however, almost entirely the result of including the catalogue of Future Foods, which is specialising in rare and unusual vegetables. For many of these, it is the only supplier.

We continue to be concerned by the number of varieties that are available from a single supplier, 53% of the open-pollinated varieties. This means that should that supplier decide to give up, the variety is likely to vanish from trade. We would urge you, other things being equal, to choose varieties that have but one source of supply.

Number of Suppliers	Open Pollinated		F1 Hybrids	
	Number	Per Cent	Number	Per Cent
1	1048	53	518	63
2-5	594	30	229	28
>5	348	17	75	9
Totals	·1990	100	822	100

As before, using *The Vegetable Finder* is simple. For every variety there is an entry that indicates whether it is open pollinated or an F1 hybrid and gives a list of suppliers. To find details of the suppliers, match the code with the entry at the back of the book. The big change in this year's edition is that it now carries descriptions. Not of all the varieties, and not unbiassed, but at least it is a start.

We have taken the descriptions, by and large, from the seed catalogues, identifying each one with its supplier code. The main exception is among the potatoes, where we have used Lawrence Hills' descriptions lifted from *The Good Potato Guide*, which is sadly no longer in print. Borrowing descriptions from the catalogues is not the ideal solution; it would be better to have available the assessments of disinterested parties, but these have so far proved impossible to obtain. Amalgamating the several, often varied, descriptions from a number of suppliers proved too time-consuming, for now. So we have adopted this as the simplest solution. If nothing else, it gives you a good idea of the diversity of descriptive styles among the different suppliers; but please do not blame me if things do not turn out as described. Sincere thanks to Patricia Carry and Rachel Pearcey for being such diligent copy typists, and Jeremy Rayner for typesetting (and missing The Archers).

By the time the next edition appears, we hope to have descriptions for everything, which we hope will make *The Vegetable Finder* even more useful than it currently is.

Finally, people often ask me what the Heritage Seed Programme of the HDRA is doing compiling a list of commercially available varieties. The answer is that we would far rather varieties continued to be available commercially, and we hope that this book, quite apart from enabling us to keep tabs on the seed trade, will enable people to find, and buy, the varieties they want. Although we maintain own Seed Library (for details of which, please write), we do not see ourselves as competitors of the big seed companies. The law, as it stands, prompts them to make economic decisions that leave gardeners unable to buy the varieties they want. Some of those – more than 200, in fact – we keep available in our Seed Library. But we would far rather see a change in the law to recognise the special needs of gardeners and small growers than continue adding to the Seed Library. *The Vegetable Finder* is one way of stimulating the demand that, we hope, will eventually lead to change.

Jeremy Cherfas
Head, HDRA Department of Genetic Resources
Ryton-on-Dunsmore, Coventry, CV8 3LG

Amaranth (Grain)
Amaranthus spp.

One of the Lost Crops of the Incas, sometimes called Quinoa. More work is probably needed before it is reliable in our climate, but well worth a try.

Burgundy
  Suppliers: Futu
Golden
  Suppliers: Futu
Multicolor
  Suppliers: Futu

Amaranth (Leaf)
Amaranthus gangeticus; also *A.dubius, A. mangostanus, A. spinosus*

Although the leaves of Grain Amaranth are edible, those of Leaf Amaranths are especially nutritious. There is great variation in leaf shape and colour. A sunny, sheltered site is of benefit.

Cahuil
  Suppliers: Futu
Dave
  Suppliers: Futu
Faro
  Suppliers: Futu
Isluga Yellow
  Suppliers: Futu
Own Strain
  Suppliers: Futu
Vegetable Amaranth
  Suppliers: Suff

Artichoke
Cynara scolymus
A relative of the thistle. It is the fleshy bracts of the unopened flower heads that are eaten, and the plants look very good in a decorative border.

Green Ball
This variety is grown for the large fleshy scales or bracts on the flower heads, which can be boiled in salted water. Young plants will produce usable heads in the second year. (Dob)
　　Suppliers: Dob

Green Globe
A gourmet variety. Harvest the large flower heads while the fleshy scales are still packed tight. Boil until tender and serve with melted butter. (Unwi)
　　Suppliers: Brwn; Butc; CGar; Chil; D&D; EWK; Foth; John; JWB; Mars; Mole; OGC; Rog; SbS; SMM; Sutt; Tuck

Green Globe Improved
With sharp spines greatly reduced and larger, heavier bearing, consistent quality globe-shaped heads, this is a much improved variety. (T&M)
　　Suppliers: T&M

Purple Globe
For those who like 'haute cuisine'. The thick, fleshy artichoke bottoms can be prepared in several ways. The globe artichoke is a very decorative garden plant that flowers beautifully with large, purple flowers. It should be planted in a sunny sheltered position and be protected in winter. (Bakk)
　　Suppliers: Bakk; Butc; CGar; EWK; OGC; Rog; SbS; VanH

Violetta di Chioggia
A luxury vegetable that is easily raised from seed. This variety produces a delicious and attractive purple headed artichoke. Decorative enough for the flower border. Select the best plants and propagate by division. (Some heads will be green from this seed). (Suff)
　　Suppliers: Suff

Asparagus
Asparagus officinalis
One of the few edible members of the Lily family. The Emperor
Augustus was very partial to asparagus, which has been grown as a
food plant since 200 BC. New all-male hybrids may be more
productive.
F1 Accell
Suppliers: EWK; OGC; Rog; SbS; SMM; Suff
F1 Andreas
Suppliers: Dob
Argenteuil Purple Imported
Suppliers: SbS
F1 Boonlim
Suppliers: RSlu; SMM; T&M
Cito
This French variety has consistently given outstanding results with yields of
over 4b per crown. Longer spears than traditional varieties that are just as
tasty and tender. A light crop may be harvested during the first year. Quite
delicious. (Foth)
Suppliers: Foth; Sutt
Connover's Colossal
This is an excellent standard variety which is an early and heavy cropper.
Being open pollinated you get more seed for your money but have to wait an
extra season for the first crop. (Suff)
Suppliers: Barb; Brwn; Butc; CGar; Chil; D&D; Dob; EWK; JWB; Mars;
Mole; OGC; Rog; SbS; SMM; Suff; Unwi; VanH; Yate
F1 Franklim
Suppliers: John; Mars; RSlu
F1 Gijnlim
Suppliers: RSlu
F1 Limbras
Suppliers: Butc; CGar; Unwi
Limburgia
Excellent asparagus with a mild flavour. Limburgia is as soft as butter and not
stringy. High yield. (Bakk)
Suppliers: Bakk
F1 Lucullus
Suppliers: Mars

Mary Washington
Suppliers: Rog; SbS; Sutt; T&M
Merrygreen
Green asparagus, very tender. Thick spears. Grows without earthing up. Very agreeable flavour. (Bakk)
Suppliers: Bakk
F1 Rekord
Suppliers: Yate
F1 Venlim
Suppliers: SMM

Asparagus Pea
Psophocarpous tetraglonobus
A member of the Legume family, with delightful brick-red flowers. The pods should be picked very small, before they toughen.

Asparagus Pea
Red flowers followed by winged pods which should be picked when about one inch long. Saute in butter and whole for a delicate, aromatic flavour with more than a hint of asparagus. Low bushy plants. (Foth)
Suppliers: Butc; CGar; Cham; Dob; EWK; Foth; Futu; JWB; OGC; SbS; SMM; T&M; Tuck

Aubergine
Solanum melongena
Also known as the eggplant, and a relative of the tomato and potato. Usually grown with some protection for reliable cropping in the U.K.

Black Beauty
Excellent, open-pollinated variety. Dark purple-black, pear-shaped fruits of good flavour. (Foth)
Suppliers: Foth; Mole; Rog; SbS
F1 Black Enorma
Suppliers: T&M
F1 Black Prince
Suppliers: T&M
F1 Black bell
Suppliers: John; Yate
F1 Bonica
Suppliers: Brwn; Dob; Foth

Claresse
  Suppliers: Cart
F1 Dobrix
  Suppliers: Toze
F1 Dusky
  Suppliers: Sutt
Easter Egg
  Suppliers: John; Unwi
F1 Elondo
  Suppliers: T&M
F1 Large Fruited Slice-Rite
  Suppliers: Mars
Little Fingers
A distinctive variety, ideal for patio-growing but also well suited for the greenhouse or a sheltered sunny area in the garden. Slender cylindrical, glossy, purple fruits are borne in clusters of 3-6. (Dob)
  Suppliers: Dob
Long Purple
Very easy to cultivate, preferably in a warm, sunny position. It will give a high yield of beautiful, purple fruit. (Bakk)
  Suppliers: Bakk; Barb; Butc; CGar; Chil; D&D; EWK; John; JWB;
  OGC; Rog; SbS; Tuck; VanH
F1 Long Tom
  Suppliers: CGar; OGC; Rog; SbS
F1 Moneymaker
  Suppliers: Butc; EWK; Foth; Mole; Rog; SbS; Sutt; Toze
New York Round Purple
  Suppliers: SbS
F1 Onita
  Suppliers: Suff
F1 Ovana
  Suppliers: Sutt
F1 Rima
  Suppliers: Bree
F1 Short Tom
  Suppliers: Rog; SbS; Suff
F1 Slice Rite
  Suppliers: Butc; Rog; SbS; Tuck

Slice Rite 23
The large, black, oblong fruits can weigh as much as 500g/1lb. Very heavy cropper. (Unwi)
   Suppliers: Unwi
F1 Vista
   Suppliers: Bakk

Basella
Basella rubra; also *B. alba, B. cordifolia*
Also known as Ceylon Spinach and Indian Spinach, the leaves, leaf stalks and stems all have a very mild spinach flavour. Very tender, it will not stand any frost, and grows much more rapidly after midsummer.
Indian Spinach
Not a variety, but an alternative name for Basella.
   Suppliers: Suff

Bean Other
Extra Early Ben Yard Long Bean
Vigna uniquiculata. Eaten as far afield as India and the West Indies, this giant, novel bean can be grown successfully in a greenhouse in the British Isles. (Foth)
   Suppliers: Foth
Gion Green Soy Bean
Gion A vigorous variety maturing early, in 75 days from sowing. The large dark green pods are picked and cooked when still green. Either eat hot like French Beans or allow to cool, shell out the seeds and eat as a snack. (OGC)
   Suppliers: OGC; SMM
Liana Asparagus Bean
A novelty item recommended for growing in a greenhouse or maybe in a warm sheltered position outside in the Southern counties. The long (15-24in.) pods are slim and best cooked cut into 1 inch pieces. The name Asparagus Bean refers to its delicious flavour. (John)
   Suppliers: John; Rog; SMM
Soya
   Suppliers: Cham

Beetroot
Beta vulgaris var. *conditiva*
Related to Swiss Chard and Mangels. Normally grown for the
swollen roots, although the leaves are also good to eat.
  Albina Vereduna
      Suppliers: T&M
  Avon Early
      Suppliers: SbS
  Barbietola di Chioggia
      Suppliers: OGC; Suff
  Bikores
      Suppliers: Brwn; John; Mole; SbS
  Boldet
      Suppliers: Toze
  Boltardy
      Suppliers: Barb; Bree; Brwn; Cart; CGar; Chil; D&D; Dob; EWK; Foth;
      John; JWB; Mars; Mole; OGC; Rog; SbS; SMM; Sutt; T&M; Toze;
      Tuck; Unwi; VanH; Yate
  Bonel
      Suppliers: Foth
  Boston
      Suppliers: Toze
  Bull's Blood
      Suppliers: Suff
  Burpees Golden
      Suppliers: Butc; CGar; Chil; D&D; Dob; EWK; John; JWB; OGC; Rog;
      SbS; Suff; Sutt; T&M; Tuck; Unwi
  Cheltenham Green Top
      Suppliers: CGar; Dob; EWK; JWB; MAS; Mole; Rog; SbS; Sutt; Toze
  Cheltenham Mono
      Suppliers: Mars; SbS; Toze
  Covent Garden
      Suppliers: SbS
  Crimson King
      Suppliers: Barb; CGar; EWK; OGC; Rog; VanH
  Cylindra
      Suppliers: Barb; Brwn; D&D; EWK; John; JWB; Mars; Rog; SbS; Suff;
      T&M; Tuck; Unwi; VanH

Detroit
Suppliers: Brwn; CGar; Chil; John; MAS; Mole; OGC; SbS; SMM; Tuck; VanH

Detroit 2
Suppliers: Barb; Cart; Dob; Mars; Sutt

Detroit 2 Little Ball
Suppliers: CGar; D&D; Dob; Foth; Mars; Rog; SbS; Sutt; VanH

Detroit 2 Nero
Suppliers: RSlu

Detroit 2 New Globe
Suppliers: Bree; Dob; Foth; SbS; Yate

Detroit 6 Rubidus
Suppliers: RSlu; T&M

Detroit Blood Red
Suppliers: SbS

Detroit Crimson
Suppliers: T&M

Detroit Crimson Globe
Suppliers: JWB

Detroit Dark Red
Suppliers: Bakk

Detroit Globe
Suppliers: EWK; Rog

Detroit Loki
Suppliers: Bakk

Detroit Slobolt
Suppliers: SbS

Dragon
Suppliers: Foth

Dwergina
Suppliers: Chil; JWB; OGC; SbS; Suff; VanH

Egyptian Turnip Rooted
Suppliers: Bakk; SbS

Forono
Suppliers: Bakk; Dob; EWK; Foth; OGC; SbS; Sutt

Golden Ball
Suppliers: SbS

Kogel
Suppliers: VanH

Kyros
  Suppliers: JWB; MAS
Libero
  Suppliers: CGar; EWK; Rog; SbS; VanH
Little Ball
  Suppliers: EWK
Mammoth Long
  Suppliers: CGar; Rob
Monaco
  Suppliers: Dob
Moneta
  Suppliers: Sutt
Monodet
  Suppliers: Mars; SbS; Toze
Monogram
  Suppliers: John; T&M; Toze; Unwi
Monopoly
  Suppliers: Bree; Cart; Dob; Foth; JWB; SbS; T&M
Nobolt
  Suppliers: SbS
F1 Pablo
  Suppliers: Sutt; Toze; VanH
Perfect
  Suppliers: John
Ran Uniball
  Suppliers: Bree
F1 Red Ace
  Suppliers: CGar; Foth; John; Rob; Sutt; Toze
Regala
  Suppliers: Unwi
Replata
  Suppliers: Mars; Mole; T&M
Spinel
  Suppliers: T&M
F1 Sprinter
  Suppliers: Yate
Synonyms
  Crimson Globe see Detroit
  Crimson Intermediate see Cylindra
  D'Egypte see Egyptian Turnip Rooted

Egyptian Flat see Egyptian Turnip Rooted
Extra Early Globe see Detroit
Globe see Detroit
Golden see Burpees Golden
Snowhite see Albina Vereduna

Broad Bean
Vicia faba
Very hardy beans, often overwintered.

Aquadulce Claudia
Very hardy variety for early Spring or Autumn sowing. Medium long pods with white beans. Ideal for freezing. (EWK)
   Suppliers: Barb; Bree; Brwn; Cart; CGar; D&D; Dob; EWK; Foth; John; JWB; Mars; MAS; Mole; OGC; Rog; RSlu; SbS; SMM; Sutt; T&M; Toze; Tuck; VanH; Yate

Aquadulce Loreta
A vigorous, early autumn or early spring sowing type. Ready 1 week before Aquadulce, producing well-filled pods with 7 delicious beans per pod. Excellent vigour and frost resistance. (T&M)
   Suppliers: T&M

Bonny Lad
This is excellent for small gardens. The plants are from 15-18in. high and produce 3 or 4 stems each bearing a cluster of smooth, 5in. long pods. (Dob)
   Suppliers: Cart; Dob

Brandy
A white seeded variety with medium small seeds bred specifically for processing, but which is also an excellent all purpose variety. Brandy has a high seed to pod ratio. (Bree)
   Suppliers: Bree

Bunyards Exhibition
Difficult to beat for all-round performance. Crops heavily with 'long-pod' beans full of flavour. Good for autumn or spring sowing. (Foth)
   Suppliers: Barb; Cart; CGar; EWK; Foth; John; MAS; Mole; OGC; Rog; SbS; SMM; Unwi; VanH

Cavalier
   Suppliers: Rog

Conqueror
Long pods widely used for exhibition. Plump beans of excellent flavour. (Sutt)
   Suppliers: Mole; Sutt

Dreadnought
Outstanding quality for late Spring sowing. Sturdy quick growing plants with good size pods. (EWK)
Suppliers: Brwn; CGar; Chil; Dob; EWK; MAS; Rog; SbS; SMM; Sutt; Yate

Exhibition Longpod
Long pods, good for general purposes. (Bree)
Suppliers: Bree

Express
Fast to mature from early spring sowings, this heavy cropper has recorded a maximum of 34 saleable pods per plant in commercial use. Good for freezing. (OGC)
Suppliers: Barb; CGar; Dob; EWK; Mars; OGC; Rog; RSlu; SbS; SMM; Suff; T&M; Toze

Feligreen
Suppliers: Mars

Futura
Suppliers: Foth

Green Longpod
A hardy green broad bean for overwinter or early use. Well filled pods with up to nine beans in each, can reach 12in. and more. (OGC)
Suppliers: OGC

Green Windsor
Large seeded with excellent flavour, this variety freezes well. (OGC)
Suppliers: Barb; D&D; EWK; John; OGC; Rog; SbS; Suff

Hylon
An outstanding variety producing pods of great length. Freezes well and highly recommended for exhibition. (Sutt)
Suppliers: Foth; JWB; Rog; Sutt; Tuck; Yate

Imperial Green Longpod
Produces pods some 15in. long, each containing up to 9 large, green beans. (Dob)
Suppliers: Dob; Foth; Rog; T&M; Toze

Imperial Green Windsor
Deep green colour, excellent cropper. (CGar)
Suppliers: CGar; Rog

Imperial White Longpod
Extremely long, broad pods containing 9 to 10 beans. Excellent for exhibition. (Mars)
Suppliers: Cart; Mars; Rog; Unwi

Imperial White Windsor
Long podded with well-filled pods. Seeds are good size. (Sutt)
    Suppliers: Rog; Sutt

Irago
    Suppliers: Toze

Ite Beryl
A well-known white seeded processing variety where it is used because of its small seeds. Beryl has few rivals for size, plant type and lateness. (Bree)
    Suppliers: Bree

Jade
Developed from Feligreen, it gives a heavy crop of light green beans which retain their colour after cooking. The smaller size of the beans makes them ideal for freezing. Sturdy plants, shorter than most, with upright pods. (Mars)
    Suppliers: Mars

Johnson's Wonderful
An early longpod type giving a heavy yield of good quality beans. (OGC)
    Suppliers: OGC; Rog; SbS

Jubilee Hysor
Up to 9 large succulent white beans much more closely packed into the pods than usual, thereby making shelling faster and easier. (Dob)
    Suppliers: Dob; Foth; Mars; Rog

Masterpiece Green Longpod
Excellent length of pod and table quality. A fine green-seeded broad bean and also excellent for deep freezing. (Sutt)
    Suppliers: Barb; Brwn; Cart; CGar; Chil; D&D; EWK; JWB; Mole; Rog; RSlu; SbS; Sutt; Tuck; Unwi; VanH; Yate

Medes
    Suppliers: Rog

Meteor
One of the earliest varieties producing a heavy crop of long pods (Length approx. 20cm.). A brown-cooking bean with the specific broad bean flavour. It is resistant to diseases. (Bakk)
    Suppliers: Bakk

Metissa
Fine-seeded broad bean. This white-flowering variety is insensitive to unfavourable weather conditions. Metissa is a strong broad bean which, in addition, offers a surprisingly high yield. (Bakk)
    Suppliers: Bakk

Minica
A high yielding Express type with 4-5 tiny beans per pod. Excellent for freezing. (OGC)
Suppliers: OGC; Rog
Red Epicure
A fine long pod of exhibition standard, with deep chestnut-crimson seeds. Some of the colour is lost in cooking, but it still retains the superb flavour. (Unwi)
Suppliers: Unwi
Reina Blanca
A valuable additional variety for Autumn sowing. (Barb)
Suppliers: Barb
Relon
Produces an abundance of long, plump pods containing an average of 8-9 green seeds of excellent quality and flavour. Of tallish habit, a vigorous and most reliable variety. (Dob)
Suppliers: Dob; Rog; Sutt
Statissa
Bronze seeded variety with true broad bean flavour. Consistently outyielded Express and other heavy yielding varieties. It averages 4 mid-size beans per 5in. pod. Early. (T&M)
Suppliers: Rog; T&M; Toze
The Sutton
A compact and bushy variety, little over 1ft high, ideal for small gardens. Excellent flavour. (Mars)
Suppliers: Barb; Brwn; CGar; D&D; EWK; Foth; John; JWB; Mars; Mole; OGC; Rog; SMM; Suff; Sutt; T&M; Tuck; Unwi; VanH
Threefold White
An excellent variety widely used by the canning and freezing industry. The pods are about 6-7in. long and the beans are smaller than most other varieties, with a white eye. It is a spring sowing variety. Height 3-3½ft. (John)
Suppliers: Bakk; John; JWB
Topic
Suppliers: Sutt
White Windsor
Will not stand frost, so must not be planted out or sown in the open until all danger of frost is past. (OGC)
Suppliers: Barb; D&D; EWK; JWB; OGC; Rog; SbS

Witkiem Major

A very fast and early variety giving large yields of long, thick pods. A little after Vroma. (Foth)

> Suppliers: CGar; D&D; EWK; Foth; Mole; Rog; T&M; Toze; Unwi; VanH

Witkiem Manita

An early maturing variety suitable for early spring sowings. (Bree)

> Suppliers: Bree; Brwn; John; OGC; Rog; Yate

Witkiem Vroma

An excellent spring sowing variety, it is early enough to crop at the same time as autumn sown varieties without lost yield. Good harvests of medium-size pods containing 5 or 6 white seeds. (Foth)

> Suppliers: Dob; Foth; Mars

Synonyms

> Acme see Masterpiece Green Longpod
> Colossal see Conqueror
> Giant Exhibition Longpod see Dreadnought
> Witkiem see Meteor

Broccoli

Brassica olearacea convar. *botrytis* Alef. var. *cymosa*

A brassica grown for the flower heads, this classification also includes calabrese and sprouting broccoli.

F1 115

> Suppliers: Bree; Yate

All Green Sprouting

> Suppliers: Barb

F1 Arcadia

> Suppliers: Bree; Yate

Autumn Calabrese

> Suppliers: Unwi

Autumn Spear

> Suppliers: Sutt

Broccoletto

> Suppliers: OGC; Suff

F1 Cape Queen

> Suppliers: SbS

F1 Caravel

> Suppliers: RSlu; T&M

F1 Citation
Suppliers: Dob
F1 Comanche
Suppliers: Bree
F1 Corvet
Suppliers: Brwn; Butc; Cart; CGar; D&D; Dob; EWK; Foth; John; JWB;
Mars; Mole; OGC; Rog; RSlu; SbS; Suff; T&M; Tuck; Unwi
F1 Cruiser
Suppliers: Mole; RSlu
F1 Dandy
Suppliers: SbS
Dandy Early
Suppliers: T&M
F1 Delicia
Suppliers: Bree
F1 Dundee
Suppliers: Yate
El Centro
Suppliers: Mars
F1 Emerald City
Suppliers: Yate
F1 Emperor
Suppliers: Foth; OGC; SbS; Toze; Tuck; Unwi; Yate
F1 Express Corona
Suppliers: Sutt
F1 Floccoli
Suppliers: T&M
F1 Green Comet
Suppliers: Barb; Brwn; Butc; EWK; Foth; JWB; Mole; Rog; SbS; SMM;
T&M
F1 Green Duke
Suppliers: JWB; SbS; Toze
Green Sprouting
Suppliers: Bakk; Bree; Butc; Cart; CGar; Chil; D&D; Dob; EWK; Foth;
John; JWB; Mole; OGC; Rog; SbS; SbS; VanH
F1 Greenbelt
Suppliers: Bree; Toze; Yate
F1 Lancelot
Suppliers: Yate

F1 Laser
Suppliers: RSlu
F1 Marathon
Suppliers: Bree; Toze; Yate
F1 Mercedes
Suppliers: Bree; JWB; Mars; OGC; SbS; Yate
Mirage
Suppliers: Suff
Morse's 4638
Suppliers: SbS
F1 Neptune
Suppliers: RSlu
Nine Star Perennial
Suppliers: Barb; Butc; CGar; Chil; Dob; EWK; Foth; JWB; Mars; Mole; Rog; SbS; Sutt; VanH
F1 Northern Dancer
Suppliers: Foth
Pacifica
Suppliers: Toze
F1 Packman
Suppliers: SbS; Toze; Yate
F1 Pirate
Suppliers: SbS
F1 Premium Crop
Suppliers: SbS; Toze
F1 Prima
Suppliers: SbS
F1 Prominence
Suppliers: Bree
Purple Cape
Suppliers: Toze; Yate
Purple Sprouting
Suppliers: CGar; Chil; D&D; EWK; John; Mole; Rog; SMM; Suff; Sutt; Unwi; VanH
Purple Sprouting Early
Suppliers: Bree; Brwn; Butc; Cart; Dob; Foth; JWB; Mars; OGC; RSlu; SbS; Toze; Tuck; Yate
Purple Sprouting Late
Suppliers: Barb; Bree; Brwn; Butc; JWB; Mars; OGC; RSlu; SbS; Suff; T&M; Toze

Ramoso
  Suppliers: Suff
Red Arrow
  Suppliers: T&M; Toze
Red Lion
  Suppliers: Toze
Romanesco
  Suppliers: Butc; Cart; CGar; D&D; Dob; EWK; JWB; Mars; OGC; Rog; SbS; Suff; Sutt; T&M; Unwi; VanH
Rosalind
  Suppliers: Cart; T&M; Toze
F1 Roxie
  Suppliers: Yate
F1 Royal Banquet
  Suppliers: Unwi
F1 SG1
  Suppliers: Bree; SbS; Toze
F1 Samurai
  Suppliers: Bree; SbS; Toze; Yate
F1 Septal SC
  Suppliers: SbS
F1 Shogun
  Suppliers: Bree; CGar; D&D; EWK; Foth; John; Mole; SbS; SMM; Toze; Tuck; Yate
F1 Skiff
  Suppliers: RSlu; SbS
F1 Southern Comet
  Suppliers: Bakk; Foth; Mole; SbS; Toze
F1 Sprinter
  Suppliers: Bree
Spurt
  Suppliers: T&M
F1 Stolto
  Suppliers: SbS
F1 Sumosun
  Suppliers: VanH
F1 Topstar
  Suppliers: Unwi
F1 Trixie
  Suppliers: T&M

F1 Vantage
  Suppliers: EWK; SbS
White Sprouting
  Suppliers: Barb; Bree; Cart; CGar; Chil; D&D; EWK; John; Mole; OGC; Rog; SMM; Suff
White Sprouting Early
  Suppliers: Butc; Foth; JWB; Mars; MAS; RSlu; SbS; Toze; Tuck; Unwi; VanH; Yate
White Sprouting Improved
  Suppliers: Sutt
White Sprouting Late
  Suppliers: Brwn; Butc; Dob; JWB; Mars; MAS; RSlu; SbS; Toze
White Star
  Suppliers: T&M; Toze
Synonyms
  De Cicco see Ramoso calabrese

Brussels Sprout

Brassica oleracea convar. *oleracea*

The sprouts are swollen buds on the stem, and a good firm soil is needed to ensure that they do not become too loose.

F1 7159
  Suppliers: Toze
F1 Achilles
  Suppliers: SbS
F1 Acropolis
  Suppliers: Mole; RSlu
F1 Adeline
  Suppliers: SbS
F1 Adonis
  Suppliers: Bree
F1 Agi-Lancelot
  Suppliers: SbS
F1 Ajax
  Suppliers: Bree
F1 Annette
  Suppliers: Yate
F1 Aries
  Suppliers: Mole; SbS

Ashwell Strain
Suppliers: JWB; SbS
Bedford
Suppliers: Dob
Bedford Blue Vein
Suppliers: CGar; EWK; JWB; Rog; SbS; Suff
Bedford Darkmar 21
Suppliers: Brwn; Foth; John; JWB; Mole; OGC; SbS; Tuck; VanH; Yate
Bedford Fillbasket
Suppliers: Barb; CGar; Chil; EWK; Rog; SbS; Suff; Sutt; VanH
Bedford Winter Harvest
Suppliers: Sutt
F1 Boxer
Suppliers: Mole; SbS
F1 Buttons
Suppliers: Foth
Cambridge No 1
Suppliers: CGar; JWB; SbS
Cambridge No 5
Suppliers: Barb; CGar; D&D; EWK; MAS; OGC; Rog; SbS; SMM
F1 Caroline
Suppliers: Bakk
F1 Cascade
Suppliers: Dob
F1 Cavalier
Suppliers: Mole; SbS; T&M; Toze
F1 Citadel
Suppliers: Barb; Cart; CGar; Dob; EWK; Foth; JWB; Rog; SbS; SMM; Sutt; T&M; VanH
F1 Claudette
Suppliers: Yate
F1 Cor Valiant
Suppliers: Barb; Bree; CGar; D&D; EWK; Mole; OGC; Rog; SbS; SMM; Toze; Tuck
F1 Corinth
Suppliers: Bree
F1 Dolmic
Suppliers: Mole; RSlu; T&M; Toze
Early Half Tall
Suppliers: Mole; OGC; SbS

F1 Edmund
Suppliers: Bree; Toze
Evesham Special
Suppliers: Barb; Brwn; CGar; Foth; John; MAS; Mole; Rog; SbS
F1 Fermesse
Suppliers: RSlu
F1 Fortress
Suppliers: Barb; D&D; EWK; Foth; Mars; OGC; Rog; SbS; SMM; Tuck; Unwi; VanH
F1 Gabion
Suppliers: RSlu; SbS
F1 Gavin
Suppliers: Bree
F1 Golfer
Suppliers: Mole; SbS
F1 Hossa
Suppliers: SbS
F1 Hunter
Suppliers: SbS
F1 Icarus
Suppliers: Bree; T&M
F1 Igor
Suppliers: Yate
F1 Jaqueline
Suppliers: Bakk
F1 Jogger
Suppliers: SbS
F1 Kundry
Suppliers: Bree
F1 Lancelot
Suppliers: Rog
F1 Lunet
Suppliers: Mole; RSlu; SbS
Mallard
Suppliers: JWB; Unwi
F1 Montgomery
Suppliers: Brwn; Mars; Toze
F1 Nicoline
Suppliers: Bakk

Noisette
Suppliers: Suff
F1 Odette
Suppliers: T&M; Toze; Yate
F1 Oliver
Suppliers: Bree; JWB; SbS; T&M; Toze
F1 Ormavon
Suppliers: Foth
F1 Ottoline
Suppliers: SbS
F1 Pallas
Suppliers: Bree
F1 Pantera
Suppliers: RSlu
F1 Peer Gynt
Suppliers: Barb; Bree; Brwn; Cart; CGar; D&D; Dob; EWK; Foth; John; JWB; Mars; Mole; OGC; Rog; SbS; SMM; Suff; T&M; Unwi; VanH
F1 Perfect Line
Suppliers: SbS
F1 Philemon
Suppliers: Bree
F1 Porter
Suppliers: SbS
F1 Predora
Suppliers: Mars; Mole; VanH
F1 Prince Marvel
Suppliers: EWK; Rog; SbS; SMM
F1 Rampart
Suppliers: Brwn; CGar; Dob; EWK; Mole; OGC; RSlu; SbS; Suff; Toze; Tuck; Unwi
F1 Rasmunda
Suppliers: SbS
F1 Richard
Suppliers: Bree; Toze
Roger
Suppliers: Bree; JWB; SbS; Toze; Unwi
Roodnerf
Suppliers: Dob
Roodnerf Early Button
Suppliers: Sutt

Roodnerf Stiekema
Suppliers: Bakk
Rous Lench
Suppliers: JWB; SbS
Rubine
Suppliers: Chil; Foth; JWB; OGC; SbS; SMM; Suff
F1 SG 2015
Suppliers: Bree
F1 SG 2016
Suppliers: Bree
F1 Saxon
Suppliers: Foth; Sutt
Seven Hills
Suppliers: Cart; D&D; EWK; Foth; OGC; Rog; SbS; VanH
F1 Sheriff
Suppliers: Mars; Mole; SbS
F1 Skios
Suppliers: Bree
F1 Smasher
Suppliers: VanH
F1 Solent
Suppliers: T&M
F1 Stabolite
Suppliers: T&M
F1 Stan
Suppliers: Rob
F1 Stephen
Suppliers: Bree; JWB
F1 Stockade
Suppliers: JWB; SbS
F1 Sultan
Suppliers: SbS
F1 Tardis
Suppliers: Bree; Toze
The Wroxton
Suppliers: SbS
F1 Titurel
Suppliers: Bree; SbS
F1 Topaz
Suppliers: SbS

F1 Topline
  Suppliers: Toze
F1 Troika
  Suppliers: Dob; Foth; John; SbS
F1 Trotter
  Suppliers: John
United
  Suppliers: Toze
F1 Welland
  Suppliers: Mars
F1 Wellington
  Suppliers: Foth; John; Toze; Unwi
F1 Widgeon
  Suppliers: Foth; JWB; Mars
F1 Zoras
  Suppliers: Bree; Toze
Synonyms
  Huizer Laat see Huizer's Late
  Red see Rubine
  Roodnerf Seven Hills see Seven Hills

Burdock

Arctium lappa

Although Burdock grows wild in Europe, in Japan and China it is cultivated as a vegetable. The long roots are the favoured part, although the young leaves can also be eaten. Gobo, often given as a variety name, is the Japanese for burdock.

Burdock
  Suppliers: Futu; Suff
A bushy, deep ;rooting biennial up to 2m tall, which has a long edible tap root which is stir-fried or added to soups and stews. The roots are best eaten while young and crips, e.g. in the summer or autumn from a spring sowing, as they tend to become woody if left in the ground too long. (Futu)
Greater
  Suppliers: Cham
Lesser
  Suppliers: Cham
Watanabe Early
  Suppliers: Chil

Cabbage

Brassica oleracea convar. *capitata*

F1 85F-14
Suppliers: Yate

F1 85F-5
Suppliers: Yate

F1 Advance
Suppliers: Toze

F1 Advantage
Suppliers: Toze

F1 Alt 8905
Suppliers: Toze

F1 Alt 8939
Suppliers: Toze

Amager
Suppliers: SbS

F1 Anton
Suppliers: Bree

April
Suppliers: Barb; Bree; CGar; EWK; JWB; Mole; Rog; SbS; Sutt; Tuck; VanH; Yate

F1 Aquila
Suppliers: SbS

F1 Arena
Suppliers: Yate

F1 Aristocrat
Suppliers: SbS; Toze

F1 Atria
Suppliers: RSlu

Avon Crest
Suppliers: JWB; SbS; Yate

F1 Barnaby
Suppliers: Yate

F1 Bartolo
Suppliers: CGar; Mole; SbS; Toze

F1 Big Ben
Suppliers: SbS

F1 Bison
Suppliers: SbS

Biwama
Suppliers: SbS
F1 Bonnet
Suppliers: SbS
Brunswick
Suppliers: EWK; Rog; SbS; SMM; VanH
Budereich
Suppliers: SbS; VanH
F1 Cape Horn
Suppliers: Bree; EWK; Foth; JWB; SbS; Yate
F1 Carnival
Suppliers: Toze
F1 Castello
Suppliers: Mars; SbS; T&M; Toze
F1 Celtic
Suppliers: Cart; Mole; Yate
F1 Charmant
Suppliers: Toze; Yate
Christmas Drumhead
Suppliers: Barb; CGar; D&D; Dob; EWK; John; JWB; Mars; Mole; OGC; Rog; SbS; SMM; Toze; Unwi; VanH
Christmas Drumhead Early
Suppliers: Sutt
F1 Clarinet
Suppliers: Bree
Coeur de Boeuf
Suppliers: Bakk
Coleslaw
Suppliers: CGar; D&D; EWK
F1 Comas
Suppliers: Yate
Copenhagen Market
Suppliers: SbS
Cotswold Queen
Suppliers: OGC; SbS; Yate
F1 Custodian
Suppliers: Mole; Yate
Decema Extra
Suppliers: SbS

Delicatesse
Suppliers: Sbs
F1 Delphi
Suppliers: Mole; RSlu; SbS
F1 Delus
Suppliers: RSlu
Derby Day
Suppliers: Brwn; CGar; EWK; Foth; JWB; Mars; Mole; Rog; SbS; Toze; Tuck; VanH; Yate
Dorado
Suppliers: SbS
F1 Dumas
Suppliers: RSlu
F1 Duncan
Suppliers: Brwn; Mole; SbS; Toze; Unwi; VanH; Yate
Durham Early
Suppliers: Barb; Brwn; CGar; EWK; Foth; JWB; Mars; MAS; Mole; Rog; SbS; Sutt; Tuck; Unwi; VanH
Durham Elf
Suppliers: Bree; John; SbS; Yate
Dutch Late Winter
Suppliers: Barb
Early Jersey Wakefield
Suppliers: Suff
Ellam's Early Dwarf
Suppliers: Barb; D&D; EWK; JWB; OGC; Rog; SbS
F1 Emerald Cross Summer Monarch
Suppliers: JWB
Enkhuizen Glory
Suppliers: SbS
F1 Erdeno
Suppliers: Bree
F1 Espoir
Suppliers: Toze; Yate
F1 Eureka
Suppliers: Yate
Express
Suppliers: Barb; Bree; Brwn; Cart; CGar; Chil; D&D; Dob; Foth; John; JWB; Mars; MAS; Mole; OGC; Rog; SbS; SMM; Suff; Sutt; Toze; Tuck; Unwi; VanH; Yate

F1 Felix
Suppliers: Foth
First Early Market 218
Suppliers: Bree; Brwn; Mole; RSlu; SbS; Toze; Unwi; Yate
First of June
Suppliers: Toze
F1 Fortune
Suppliers: EWK; SbS
F1 Freshma
Suppliers: SbS; Toze; Yate
F1 Garant
Suppliers: Yate
Golden Acre
Suppliers: Bakk; Barb; Brwn; CGar; Chil; D&D; Dob; EWK; Foth; John;
JWB; Mars; MAS; Mole; OGC; Rog; SbS; SMM; Sutt; Toze; Tuck;
Unwi; VanH; Yate
Golden Acre Baseball
Suppliers: SbS
Golden Acre Earliana
Suppliers: John
Golden Acre Earliest of All
Suppliers: SbS; Suff
Golden Acre Extra Early
Suppliers: Mole
Golden Acre Extra Glory
Suppliers: SbS
Golden Acre May Express
Suppliers: SbS; Sutt
Golden Acre Progress
Suppliers: Bree; SbS
Golden Acre Rapidity
Suppliers: SbS
F1 Golden Cross
Suppliers: Bree; JWB; Mole; SbS; Toze
F1 Goodma
Suppliers: Yate
F1 Green Boy
Suppliers: SbS
F1 Green Coronet
Suppliers: EWK; SbS

F1 Green Express
  Suppliers: SbS; Toze; Yate
Green Sleeves
  Suppliers: Toze
Green Wonder
  Suppliers: SbS
F1 Grenadier
  Suppliers: Bree
Greyhound
  Suppliers: EWK
Harbinger
  Suppliers: Barb; John; SbS; Suff
F1 Hawke
  Suppliers: Dob; JWB; SbS; Sutt
Herald
  Suppliers: T&M
Hercules
  Suppliers: T&M
F1 Hermes
  Suppliers: RSlu
F1 Hidena
  Suppliers: JWB; SbS; Toze
Hispi
  Suppliers: Bakk; Barb; Brwn; Cart; CGar; D&D; Dob; EWK; Foth; John; JWB; Mole; Rog; SbS; SMM; Sutt; T&M; Toze; Tuck; Unwi
F1 Histona
  Suppliers: VanH
Holland Late Winter
  Suppliers: CGar; EWK; Foth; OGC; Rog; SbS; Sutt; Tuck
Holland Winter
  Suppliers: Bakk; JWB
F1 Horizon
  Suppliers: RSlu
F1 Hornet
  Suppliers: Bree; Toze
F1 Hornspi
  Suppliers: SbS
F1 Hyjula
  Suppliers: Mole

Jersey Wakefield
Suppliers: Bree; SbS; Toze
Jupiter
Suppliers: SbS
F1 King Greens
Suppliers: RSlu
F1 Kingspi
Suppliers: Mars
F1 Krautman
Suppliers: Bakk
Langedijk 3 Starkwinter
Suppliers: Toze
Langedijk 4
Suppliers: Brwn; John; Mars; SbS; Toze; Unwi; VanH
Langedijk 4 Decema
Suppliers: Mole; SbS
Lincoln Imp
Suppliers: SbS
F1 Marathon
Suppliers: Bree; SbS
F1 Market Prize
Suppliers: SbS
Marner Allfruh
Suppliers: EWK; OGC; SbS; Yate
Marner Rocco
Suppliers: SbS
F1 Marquis Greens
Suppliers: RSlu
F1 Marvellon
Suppliers: T&M
F1 Metino
Suppliers: RSlu
F1 Metis
Suppliers: RSlu
F1 Mighty Globe
Suppliers: EWK; Rog; SMM
F1 Minicole
Suppliers: Barb; Brwn; CGar; D&D; Dob; EWK; Foth; John; JWB; Mole; OGC; Rog; SbS; SMM; Suff; Sutt; T&M; Tuck; Unwi; VanH

F1 Musketeer
Suppliers: Bree
Myatts Early Offenham
Suppliers: JWB
Niggerhead
Suppliers: SbS
Noblesse
Suppliers: SbS
Offenham
Suppliers: EWK; OGC; Rog; SMM
Offenham 1 Little Kempsey
Suppliers: SbS
Offenham 1 Myatts Offenham Compacta
Suppliers: Bree; Brwn; Mars; RSlu; SbS; Toze; Yate
Offenham 2 First and Best
Suppliers: SbS
Offenham 2 Flower of Spring
Suppliers: Barb; CGar; Chil; D&D; Dob; EWK; Foth; John; JWB; Mole; OGC; Rog; SbS; SMM; Sutt; Toze; Tuck
Offenham 3 Kempsey
Suppliers: SbS; Yate
Offenham 3 Wintergreen
Suppliers: Bree; CGar; EWK; JWB; Mars; OGC; Rog; RSlu; SbS; Suff; Toze; Tuck; Yate
Offenham BG 283
Suppliers: SbS
Offenham Early Selected
Suppliers: Barb
Offenham Hardy Offenham
Suppliers: Toze
F1 Oscar
Suppliers: Foth
F1 Patron
Suppliers: T&M
F1 Pedrillo
Suppliers: John; SbS; Toze
F1 Perfect Ball
Suppliers: T&M
Pewa
Suppliers: Yate

F1 Picolo
Suppliers: Toze
F1 Pict
Suppliers: Bree
F1 Piton
Suppliers: Bree
Pixie
Suppliers: Brwn; Mars; Sutt; T&M; Toze; Unwi
F1 Polestar
Suppliers: SbS
F1 Polinius
Suppliers: Mars; SbS; Toze
F1 Primata
Suppliers: SbS
Primax
Suppliers: SbS
F1 Prince Greens
Suppliers: RSlu
F1 Princess
Suppliers: SbS
F1 Prospera
Suppliers: Brwn; EWK; Mole; SbS
F1 Puma
Suppliers: Toze; Yate
F1 Quickstep
Suppliers: Mars; T&M
F1 Quisto
Suppliers: Bree
F1 Ramco
Suppliers: Bree
F1 Rapid
Suppliers: SbS
F1 Rapier
Suppliers: Dob; SbS; T&M
F1 Renova
Suppliers: SbS
F1 Riana
Suppliers: EWK; SbS
F1 Rinda
Suppliers: RSlu

Robinsons Champion
Suppliers: CGar; JWB; MAS; Rob; SbS
F1 Rodeo
Suppliers: SbS
F1 Rodon
Suppliers: SbS
F1 SG 2810
Suppliers: Bree
F1 SG 2811
Suppliers: Bree
F1 SG 2812
Suppliers: Bree
F1 SG 3010
Suppliers: Bree
F1 Sagitta
Suppliers: RSlu
F1 Scanvi
Suppliers: Yate
F1 Slawdena
Suppliers: SbS; Toze
F1 Sparkel
Suppliers: Dob; Foth
F1 Sphinx
Suppliers: RSlu
F1 Spitfire
Suppliers: Dob; Foth; Mole; OGC; SbS; Toze
F1 Spivoy
Suppliers: Foth; T&M
F1 Spring Hero
Suppliers: Barb; CGar; D&D; Dob; EWK; Foth; John; JWB; Mars; Mole; OGC; Rog; SbS; SMM; Tuck; Unwi; Yate
Standby
Suppliers: SbS; Toze
Starski
Suppliers: Yate
F1 Stetson
Suppliers: Bree
F1 Stonehead
Suppliers: Bree; Brwn; CGar; Dob; Foth; JWB; Mole; OGC; SbS; Toze; Yate

F1 Supergreen
Suppliers: SbS
F1 Trumpet
Suppliers: Bree
Volga
Suppliers: Mole
Wheelers Imperial
Suppliers: Brwn; Cart; CGar; Chil; Dob; EWK; John; JWB; Mole; Rog; SbS; SMM; Sutt; Tuck; Yate
Wheelers Imperial Early Queen
Suppliers: SbS; Suff
Wiam
Suppliers: Mars; Mole; SbS; Unwi
Winnigstadt
Suppliers: Barb; CGar; Chil; D&D; Dob; EWK; Foth; John; JWB; Mars; MAS; Mole; OGC; Rog; SbS; Suff; Sutt; Tuck; VanH
Witham Wonder Springtime
Suppliers: SbS
Synonyms
Alpha see Golden Acre
Brunswijker see Brunswick
Ditmarscher Forcing see Golden Acre
Early Drumhead see Brunswick
Early Flat Dutch see Brunswick
Express see Greyhound
Gloria see Green Boy
Gouden Akker see Golden Acre
Greyhound see Express
Holland Winter E50 see Langedijk 4
Holland Winter White Extra Late see Langedijk 4
Improved Hispi see Kingspi
June Giant see Golden Acre
June Star see Princess
Late Winter Giant see Langedijk 4
Offenham Compacta see Offenham 1 Myatts Offenham Compacta
Primo see Golden Acre
Roem van Enkhuizen see Enkhuizen Glory
Steenkop see Stonehead
Summer Monarch see Emerald Cross
Vienna see Green Wonder
Winnigstadter see Winnigstadt

Wintergreen see Offenham 3 Wintergreen

Cabbage Abyssinian
Karate
Suppliers: Cham

Cabbage Chinese Headed
Brassica rapa var. *pekinensis*
Chinese cabbage comes in two basic varieties, headed and loose-headed. The names of varieties still need further sorting out. Some varieties are very susceptible to bolting, and it is important to choose appropriate varieties and sow at the correct time.
F1 Chiko
Suppliers: John
Chin Suan
Suppliers: Bakk
F1 China Express
Suppliers: EWK; SbS
F1 China King 14
Suppliers: Chil
F1 China Pride
Suppliers: Sutt
F1 Chirimen
Suppliers: Foth; Yate
F1 Eskimo
Suppliers: Dob; Suff
F1 Festival
Suppliers: John
F1 Green Rocket
Suppliers: SbS
F1 Harmony
Suppliers: Sutt; Yate
F1 Hopkin
Suppliers: Bree
F1 Hypro
Suppliers: RSlu
F1 Jade Pagoda
Suppliers: Toze; Yate

F1 Kasumi
Suppliers: Mars; Toze; Yate
Lei-choi
Suppliers: Butc
F1 Mariko
Suppliers: T&M
Market Pride
Suppliers: Chil
Michihili
Suppliers: SbS
F1 Monument
Suppliers: Bakk
F1 Nagaoka
Suppliers: Brwn; SbS; Toze
F1 Nagaoka 50 Days
Suppliers: Mole
F1 Nagaoka 60 day
Suppliers: Foth
F1 Nerva
Suppliers: Bakk
Pe-tsai
Not a variety name.
  Suppliers: Barb; Butc; CGar; D&D; EWK; OGC; SbS; VanH
Round Leaved Santo
Suppliers: Chil
Santo
Suppliers: SbS
Serrated Leaved Santo
Suppliers: Chil; Suff
F1 Shanghai
Suppliers: Suff
Shantung
Suppliers: Chil
F1 Tako
Suppliers: Yate
F1 Tango
Suppliers: Yate
F1 Tip Top
Suppliers: Butc; Cart; John; JWB; OGC; SbS; Tuck

F1 Tip Top 12
Suppliers: Chil
F1 Tip Top China Express
Suppliers: Bakk; CGar; Toze
F1 Tonkin
Suppliers: Bree
Tsai Shim
Suppliers: Chil
Tsoisam
Suppliers: Suff
F1 WR 60 Days
Suppliers: SbS
F1 WR 70 Days
Suppliers: SbS
WR 85 Days
Suppliers: Sbs
Synonyms
Early Jade Pagoda see Michihili
Wong Bok see Pe-tsai

Cabbage Other
Couve Tronchuda
Suppliers: Chil
Jersey Walking Stick
Suppliers: Chil; Foth; T&M

Cabbage Red
Brassica oleracea convar. *capitata*
F1 Autoro
Suppliers: John; SbS; Toze
F1 Hardoro
Suppliers: EWK; OGC; SbS
Langedijk Red Late
Suppliers: Bakk; Sbs
Langedijk Red Medium
Suppliers: Dob; SbS
Langedijk Red Red King
Suppliers: VanH
Mammoth Red Rock
Suppliers: Brwn

F1 Rebus
Suppliers: Bree
Red Drumhead 2
Suppliers: Bakk; Barb; CGar; Chil; D&D; EWK; John; JWB; Mars; Mole; OGC; Rog; SMM; Sutt; T&M; Tuck; VanH
Red Kissendrup
Suppliers: Toze
Red Meteor
Suppliers: Toze
F1 Redar
Suppliers: Bree
F1 Revue
Suppliers: Bree
F1 Rodima
Suppliers: Yate
F1 Rona
Suppliers: RSlu
F1 Rookie
Suppliers: Foth; Yate
F1 Roxy
Suppliers: RSlu
F1 Ruby Ball
Suppliers: Bakk; Foth; JWB; Mars; SbS; Suff; Unwi; Yate
F1 Ruby Perfection
Suppliers: Bakk
F1 Vorox
Suppliers: RSlu
Synonyms
Langedijk Red Autumn see Langedijk Red Medium
Langedijker Bewaar see Langedijk Red Late
Langedijker Herfst see Langedijk Red Medium
Red Dutch see Red Drumhead
Red King see Langedijk Red
Roodkop see Red Drumhead

Cabbage Savoy
F1 Alaska
Suppliers: Bree
Alexanders No 1
Suppliers: Mars; SbS

Alexanders No 1 Lincoln Late
Suppliers: SbS
F1 Aquarius
Suppliers: John; JWB
Avon Coronet
Suppliers: SbS
Best Of All
Suppliers: Brwn; Cart; Dob; EWK; JWB; Mole; SbS; Sutt; Tuck
F1 Bingo
Suppliers: Brwn
F1 Celsa
Suppliers: Bakk; SbS
F1 Celtic
Suppliers: Barb; Brwn; CGar; Dob; EWK; Foth; JWB; Mars; OGC; Rog; SbS; SMM; Sutt; Toze; Tuck; Unwi; VanH
F1 Concerto
Suppliers: Yate
F1 Corsair
Suppliers: Dob; SbS
F1 Hamasa
Suppliers: Bakk; SbS
Hammer Herba
Suppliers: Mole
F1 Ice Queen
Suppliers: Barb; CGar; D&D; EWK; SbS; SMM; Tuck; Unwi; VanH
F1 Icecap
Suppliers: Bree
January King
Suppliers: Barb; Brwn; CGar; Chil; EWK; Foth; John; JWB; Mars; OGC; Rog; SbS; SMM; T&M; Unwi; VanH
January King Hardy Late Stock 3
Suppliers: Bree; Cart; Dob; Mars; Mole; RSlu; SbS; Sutt; Toze; Tuck; Yate
January King Improved Extra Late
Suppliers: SbS
January King Improved Late
Suppliers: SbS
F1 Julius
Suppliers: Bree; Dob; T&M; Toze

Late Drumhead
Suppliers: JWB; SbS
F1 Lucetta
Suppliers: John
F1 Marabel
Suppliers: SbS; Toze
Marner Julico
Suppliers: SbS
Marner Lagerweiss
Suppliers: SbS
Marner Sepco
Suppliers: SbS
F1 Mila
Suppliers: Bree
F1 Morgan
Suppliers: Brwn
Novum
Suppliers: SbS
F1 Novusa
Suppliers: Mars; Toze
Ormskirk
Suppliers: D&D; EWK; OGC; VanH
Ormskirk 1 Ormskirk Late
Suppliers: Barb; Brwn; Chil; Dob; John; Mars; SbS; Suff
Ormskirk 1 Rearguard
Suppliers: Sutt
Ormskirk Early
Suppliers: SbS
Ormskirk Extra Late
Suppliers: Mole; SbS; Tuck
Ormskirk Late Drumhead
Suppliers: Unwi
Ormskirk Medium
Suppliers: SbS
F1 Paressa
Suppliers: Toze
Perfection Drumhead
Suppliers: Barb; EWK; SbS
F1 Prelude
Suppliers: Yate

F1 Protovoy
  Suppliers: Dob
F1 Rhapsody
  Suppliers: Yate
F1 Saga
  Suppliers: RSlu
F1 Salarite
  Suppliers: Bakk
Savoy King
  Suppliers: Foth; Unwi
F1 Silva
  Suppliers: Foth; Sutt
F1 Sindria
  Suppliers: RSlu
Starski
  Suppliers: CGar; EWK; OGC; SbS; Tuck
F1 Stilon
  Suppliers: RSlu
F1 Taler
  Suppliers: Mars; RSlu
F1 Tarvoy
  Suppliers: EWK; SbS; T&M
F1 Tasmania
  Suppliers: Bree; Brwn
F1 Tombola
  Suppliers: SbS; Tuck
F1 Tundra
  Suppliers: Brwn; Dob; Mars; Mole; OGC; SbS; T&M; Toze; Yate
Vertus
  Suppliers: Bakk
Winter King
  Suppliers: Bakk; Mars; SbS; Sutt; Toze; VanH
Winter King Harda
  Suppliers: Mole; Suff
Winter King Shortie
  Suppliers: SbS
F1 Winter Star
  Suppliers: SbS
F1 Winterton
  Suppliers: Brwn; John; Sutt; Toze

F1 Wintessa
   Suppliers: SbS; Toze
F1 Wirosa
   Suppliers: Brwn; JWB; Mole; Toze; Tuck; VanH; Yate
F1 Wivoy
   Suppliers: Dob; Mars; SbS; Toze
F1 Yslanda
   Suppliers: SbS
Synonyms
   De Pontoise 3 see January King
   Herfstgroene see Novum

Camas
Camassia quamash
A native of North America, the bulbs are eaten.
   Camas
      Suppliers: Futu

Cape Gooseberry
Physalis peruviana
Related to tomatoes, the deliciously aromatic edible fruits are enclosed in papery lanterns.
   Cape Gooseberry
      Suppliers: Butc; Dob; John; OGC; SMM; Sutt
   Golden Berry
      Suppliers: Foth; T&M; Unwi
   Pineapple Cherry
      Suppliers: Bakk

Cardoon
Cynara cardunculus
Very similar to artichokes, but it is the blanched stems, rather than the flowers, that are eaten.
   Cardoon
      Suppliers: Butc; CGar; Cham; Chil; EWK; JWB; OGC; SbS; SMM
   Gigante di Romagna
      Suppliers: Suff

Carrot

Daucus carota

F1 Almaro
Suppliers: RSlu; T&M

Amsterdam Forcing 3
Early carrot, extremely suitable for sowing early in a cold frame. Good for cultivation in the open. (Bakk)

Suppliers: Bakk; Brwn; CGar; D&D; Dob; EWK; Foth; JWB; Mars; Mole; OGC; Rog; SbS; Sutt; Toze; Tuck

Amsterdam Forcing Caramba
Suppliers: Bree

Amsterdam Sweetheart
This is the variety to grow if you love the flavour of young 'Finger Carrots'! Pull them as young as possible, and enjoy their superb sweet flavour. Splendid for freezing - so none need be wasted. (Unwi)

Suppliers: Unwi

F1 Anglia
Suppliers: Bree

Astra
Suppliers: EWK

Autumn King
A true winter carrot: robust vegetable, producing a heavy carrot which is, however, fairly smooth. It has a beautiful colour inside and outside. (Bakk)

Suppliers: Bakk; CGar; Chil; D&D; EWK; Foth; John; JWB; MAS; Mole; OGC; Rog; SbS; SMM; Sutt; Unwi

Autumn King 2
Suppliers: Cart; Dob

Autumn King 2 Vita Longa
Suppliers: Brwn; Foth; Mars; SbS; Suff

Autumn King Giganta
Suppliers: SMM

Autumn King Improved
Reliable heavy yielding main crop for eating fresh, winter storage or freezing. (T&M)

Suppliers: SbS; T&M; Tuck

Autumn King Red Winter
Suppliers: Barb; SbS

Autumn King Trophy
Suppliers: Bree

Autumn King Viking
Suppliers: SbS
F1 Bangor
Suppliers: Sutt
Banta
Sturdy, well coloured roots with high carotene content. Heavy top for good protection and easy lifting. (EWK)
Suppliers: EWK; SbS
Beacon
A British bred maincrop variety producing uniform long slightly tapered roots. Gives a heavy yield and in trials has gained top ratings for both flesh and core colour. Flavour first-class. (Sutt)
Suppliers: Sutt
Bercoro
Suppliers: RSlu
Berlicum
Beautiful, cylindrical, stump-rooted, red winter carrot. Narrow core. Fine flavour. (Bakk)
Suppliers: Bakk; EWK; SbS; T&M
F1 Berlicum 2 Berjo
Suppliers: Mars; Mole; SbS; Suff; Toze; Yate
Berlicum Oranza
Maincrop type of good core and flesh colour. Roots are almost cylindrical and of very high quality. Suitable for harvest from August to Christmas. Mid-season. (Brwn)
Suppliers: Brwn; SbS
Berlicum Special
Suppliers: SbS
F1 Berlina
Suppliers: Yate
F1 Bernova
Suppliers: Bakk; SbS
F1 Bertan
Suppliers: T&M
F1 Bertop
Suppliers: Bree; T&M
F1 Bingo
Suppliers: Yate
Bridge
Suppliers: SbS

F1 Butor
Suppliers: Toze
Camberley
A high quality half-long maincrop. Tapered roots are usually 7-9in. (17-23cm.) long with a deep orange colour and a smooth skin. Used for overwintering, particularly in heavy soils, and recommended for both commercial and garden use. (OGC)
Suppliers: OGC
Campestra
An exceptionally good Autumn King type of appetising deep orange-red. The roots from 6-8in. long, are strong shouldered, slightly tapered and cylindrical. For use during autumn and early winter. (Dob)
Suppliers: CGar; Dob; SbS
F1 Camus
Suppliers: Dob
F1 Cardinal
Suppliers: Dob
Chanson
Suppliers: RSlu
Chantenay
A maincrop variety, giving a thick, medium length, stump-rooted carrot. It stores well and is suited to a late summer sowing. (John)
Suppliers: John
Chantenay Babycan
Ideal for the production of baby carrots. Seed may be broadcast to provide up to 45 plants per square foot. Develops fast. Rich coloured with little core and great flavour. (Suff)
Suppliers: Suff
Chantenay Canners Favourite
Suppliers: Yate
Chantenay Long
Suppliers: Yate
Chantenay Red Cored
A stump-rooted, early maincrop with small cored orange roots of fine texture. (Dob)
Suppliers: Barb; Bree; Cart; CGar; Chil; D&D; Dob; EWK; JWB; MAS; Mole; OGC; Rog; SbS; SMM; Toze; Unwi; VanH
Chantenay Red Cored 2
Suppliers: Mars
Chantenay Red Cored 3 Supreme
Suppliers: SbS; T&M

Chantenay Red Cored Fenman
Suppliers: SbS
Chantenay Royal
A stump rooted main crop variety excellent in any soil and ideal for clay.
Rich coloured roots and fine flavour. (Suff)
Suppliers: Barb; Bree; Brwn; EWK; Rog; SbS; Suff; Tuck
F1 Cobba
Suppliers: Dob; Yate
F1 Condor
Suppliers: Bree
F1 Coronet
Suppliers: SbS
Danvers Half Long Danvers 126
Suppliers: SbS
Danvers Scarlet Intermediate
Suppliers: SbS
Decora
Fast growing Nantes type with very smooth, heavy yielding roots. (EWK)
Suppliers: EWK; SbS
F1 Disco
Suppliers: Yate
F1 Dragon
Suppliers: Toze
Duke
Suppliers: SbS
Early French Frame
Quick-maturing round roots up to 50mm (about 2in.) in diameter. Ideal for
forcing or for sowing in succession outdoors. (Sutt)
Suppliers: JWB; SbS; Suff; Sutt
Early Horn
Suppliers: Foth; John; JWB; SbS; Unwi
Early Market
An early, stump-rooted variety of excellent quality, ideal for both early and
late sowing. (John)
Suppliers: Barb; D&D; EWK; John; Rog; Tuck
Fakkell Mix
Suppliers: SbS
Fancy
Suppliers: SbS

F1 Favor
Suppliers: Toze
Favourite
One of the most popular stump-rooted maincrop varieties. Excellent quality and recommended for exhibition in 'short' classes. (Sutt)
. Suppliers: Sutt
Fedora
Suppliers: SbS; Unwi
Fincor
Suppliers: RSlu
F1 Flacino
Suppliers: RSlu
Flak
Suppliers: CGar; VanH
Flakkee
Maincrop variety, large roots, excellent for the show bench. (JWB)
Suppliers: JWB
F1 Flamant
Suppliers: T&M
F1 Flex
Suppliers: Bakk
Foxey
Suppliers: SbS
F1 Gregory
Suppliers: Bree; T&M
F1 Gringo
Suppliers: Yate
Ideal
This new, fast maturing Nantes-type carrot is superb when eaten whole or grated in salads. The rich orange roots are uniform in colour and have a delicious flavour. (Dob)
Suppliers: Dob
Imperator
Suppliers: SbS
F1 Ingot
Suppliers: Foth; Unwi
F1 Ivor
Suppliers: Toze

James Scarlet Intermediate
A good early maincrop variety, with symmetrical and well tapered roots. It is well coloured and is of a good texture, making it an ideal carrot for culinary purposes. (John)
 Suppliers: Barb; CGar; Chil; D&D; EWK; Foth; John; JWB; OGC; Rog; SbS; Tuck; Unwi; VanH

F1 Jasper
 Suppliers: Dob

Juared
A medium-early to medium-late variety, so it is not a true winter carrot. Juared is sometimes called the 'health carrot', as it has the highest carotene content. Extremely rich in vitamin A. (Bakk)
 Suppliers: Bakk; John; T&M

Jumbo
 Suppliers: T&M

Karotan
Long, stump-ended roots of large size for maincrop use. Excellent flavour with high juice content. (RSlu)
 Suppliers: John; SbS

Kundulus
Window boxes, difficult soils, frames, small gardens. Very fast growing. (T&M)
 Suppliers: Cart; T&M

F1 Laranda
 Suppliers: T&M

Laros
 Suppliers: SbS

F1 Liberno
 Suppliers: RSlu; T&M

Lobbericher
A sweet, yellow fodder carrot for cattle and rabbits, goats etc. Can be stored in a pit. (Bakk)
 Suppliers: Bakk

F1 Lynx
 Suppliers: Bree

F1 Major
 Suppliers: Toze

Minicor
Excellent flavour and colours up early. Uniform 6-7in. Very slender roots. Best for 'Baby carrots'. A gourmet variety. (Suff)
 Suppliers: RSlu; Suff

F1 Mokum
Suppliers: Bakk; Cart; T&M; VanH
F1 Nabora
Suppliers: Yate
F1 Nairobi
Suppliers: Brwn
F1 Nanco
Suppliers: John; JWB; SbS
F1 Nandor
Suppliers: CGar; Rob; Toze
Nantes
Half-long, stump ended roots. Strong grower of first class quality and flavour. (EWK)
Suppliers: CGar; D&D; EWK; Foth; John; JWB; MAS; Mole; SMM; Suff; Tuck; Unwi; VanH; Barb; Rog
Nantes 2
Suppliers: Mars
Nantes 2 Ideal
Suppliers: SbS
Nantes 5
Suppliers: Cart; Sutt
Nantes 5 Champion Scarlet Horn
A fast maturing carrot of uniform shape and quality. (Dob)
Suppliers: Dob; Sutt
Nantes Express
Early maincrop. Suitable for early sowing in frames. Some cavity spot resistance. (T&M)
Suppliers: T&M; Unwi
Nantes Forto
Sweet tasting cylindrical, long and smooth skinned carrots from this improved Nantes type. Even on heavy soils this is very productive. (Foth)
Suppliers: Foth
Nantes Fruhbund
It colours very early and is, therefore, suitable for sowing early. A carrot with a good colour in- and outside, and with a very agreeable flavour. Recommended selection from the well-known Nantes group. (Bakk)
Suppliers: Bakk
Nantes Half Long
A well-known variety, popular for its high yields and its agreeable, sweet flavour. Nantes is a real summer carrot! (Bakk)
Suppliers: Bakk

F1 Nantes Nanthya
    Suppliers: Bree
Nantes Romosa
A half-long stump rooted early, excellent for forcing or outside sowing. Has very little core. A really succulent variety. First early. (Brwn)
    Suppliers: Brwn
F1 Narante
    Suppliers: Bakk
F1 Narman
    Suppliers: Mole; SbS; VanH
F1 Navarre
    Suppliers: Foth
F1 Nelson
    Suppliers: Sutt
New Radiance
    Suppliers: SbS
Oxheart Guerande
A very old variety, with broad shoulders, stump rooted and early with a fine flavour. (Suff)
    Suppliers: SbS; Suff
Panther
    Suppliers: Bree; Unwi
Parabell
    Suppliers: SbS
Parmex
    Suppliers: Dob; Foth; John
F1 Primo
    Suppliers: Mars
F1 Punta
    Suppliers: Yate
F1 Rapier
    Suppliers: Toze
Red Chantenay
    Suppliers: JWB
Red Intermediate
Useful stump-rooted type for both early and maincrop use. (Barb)
    Suppliers: EWK
Red Intermediate Stump Rooted
    Suppliers: Barb; CGar; Rog

F1 Red Rum
Suppliers: Foth
Redca
Suppliers: OGC
F1 Redco
Suppliers: Yate
Rocket
Suppliers: Dob; Toze
Romosa
Suppliers: SbS
Rondo
Produces almost round shaped roots. Very early, uniform and sweet tasting. Easy to clean and cook whole. (EWK)
Suppliers: CGar; EWK; Mars; OGC; Rog
Royal Chantenay 2 Gold King
Suppliers: SbS
Royal Chantenay 2 No 85
Suppliers: SbS
Rubin
An early, round carrot with a good inside colour and narrow core, contrary to most other ball-shaped carrots. A variety for the professional as well as for the amateur vegetable grower. (Bakk)
Suppliers: Bakk; SbS
Rusty
Suppliers: SbS
Scarlet Nantes
Suppliers: SbS
F1 Senior
Suppliers: Toze
F1 Sheila
Suppliers: Yate
St Valery
A pre 1880 variety from France with sweet tender flesh. For best results grow this carrot in a rich deep soil where it can attain a size of 2-3in. x 12in! (Suff)
Suppliers: Barb; CGar; Chil; D&D; Dob; EWK; Foth; John; JWB; Mars; OGC; Rog; SbS; SMM; Suff; Sutt; Tuck; VanH
St Valery Special Selection
Long tapered roots, very uniform and good colour. (Rob)
Suppliers: Rob

Suko
One of the earliest sweetest little carrots we know. Recommended where space is limited also shallow or heavy soils. (T&M)
Suppliers: T&M
Sytan
This Nantes type carrot is less susceptible to carrot fly maggot than other varieties. (Mars)
Suppliers: Mars
F1 Tam-tam
Suppliers: Yate
F1 Tamino
Suppliers: Barb; CGar; D&D; EWK; John; OGC; Rog; SbS; Tuck
F1 Tancar
Suppliers: Toze
F1 Tardia
Suppliers: Bree
Tip Top
Nantes type, very good colour and quality. (JWB)
Suppliers: Bree; Dob; JWB; OGC; SbS; VanH
Titan
A Nantes type selection bred for uniformity, good shape and bright colouring with a high vitamin A content. A good resistance to cracking. (Foth)
Suppliers: Foth
Top Score
Suppliers: SbS
Touchon
A well-known variety which remotely resembles Nantes. Excellent flavour and good colour. Just like Nantes a true summer carrot. (Bakk)
Suppliers: Bakk
Touchon Ideal Red
An old French variety (pre 1880) with a fine texture and superb flavour at any size. Will grow to 8in. (20cm.). The best juicy carrot. Special improved selection. Maincrop. (Suff)
Suppliers: Suff; Toze
F1 Turbo
Suppliers: Yate
Waltham Hicolour
Suppliers: SbS
White Fodder
Don't be put off by the name. A superb mild tasting carrot very much appreciated in France. Very easy to grow and remains deliciously tender even

when very large. This is a safe carrot to eat for those allergic to carotene. (Suff)

    Suppliers: Suff

Synonyms

    Amsterdam Bak see Amsterdam Forcing 3
    Amsterdam Forcing see Amsterdam Forcing 3
    Amsterdam Outdoor see Amsterdam Forcing 3
    Chantenay a Coeur Rouge see Chantenay Red Cored
    Chantenay Model Red Cored see Chantenay Red Cored
    D'Amsterdam a Forcer see Amsterdam Forcing 3
    De Colmar a Coeur Rouge see Autumn King
    Early Market Horn see Chantenay Red Cored
    Early Nantes see Nantes
    Early Scarlet Horn see Early Horn
    First Pull see Amsterdam Forcing 3
    Juwarot see Juared
    Long Red Surrey see St Valery
    New Red Intermediate see St Valery
    Norfolk Giant see Autumn King
    Parisje Markt see Early French Frame
    Red Intermediate Stump Rooted see Chantenay Red Cored
    Saint-Valery see St Valery

Cauliflower

Brassica oleracea convar. *botrytis* Alef. var. *botrytis*

    F1 AY 575
        Suppliers: Yate
    Ace Early
        Suppliers: Dob
    Adams Early White
        Suppliers: SbS
    Alban
        Suppliers: Yate
    Alice Springs
        Suppliers: SbS
    All The Year Round

Can be sown in late autumn or spring to produce reliable, large, white heads from late June to October. (Foth)

    Suppliers: Barb; Cart; CGar; Chil; D&D; Dob; EWK; Foth; John; JWB; Mars; Mole; OGC; Rog; SMM; Suff; Sutt; T&M; Unwi; VanH; Yate

Alpha
Very popular for early work, June/July. (JWB)
    Suppliers: JWB
Alpha 5
    Suppliers: Mars; Sutt
Alpha Fortados
    Suppliers: RSlu
Alverda
    Suppliers: Bakk; Suff
Andes
This is a versatile variety for cutting in summer and autumn. Sowings can be made under glass in January-February for early crops or can be sown outdoors in a seedbed in April-May in the normal manner. Very compact in growth with excellent quality deep white curds. (Sutt)
    Suppliers: Sutt
Angers No 1
Specially recommended for Southern and Western regions. Unsuitable for cold or exposed areas. All have pure white, solid curds. Heads January-February. (Sutt)
    Suppliers: SbS; Sutt
Angers No 2
Matures February-March. (Sutt)
    Suppliers: Mars; SbS; Sutt; Unwi
Angers No 3
    Suppliers: SbS
Angers No 4
    Suppliers: SbS
Angers No 5
    Suppliers: SbS
Aprilex
    Suppliers: Bree; SbS; Yate
F1 Arbon
    Suppliers: RSlu; Toze
F1 Arcade
    Suppliers: RSlu
F1 Arfak
    Suppliers: RSlu
Armado
    Suppliers: RSlu

Armado April
Superb quality heads of pure white and large size. Cutting late April. (EWK)
    Suppliers: EWK
Armado Clio
    Suppliers: SbS; Toze
Armado Quick
    Suppliers: John; SbS
Armel 2
We can confidently recommend this variety for any part of the United
Kingdom. Truly exceptional curds and above all robust and reliable. (T&M)
    Suppliers: Yate
F1 Armetta
    Suppliers: Bakk; RSlu
Arminda
    Suppliers: Mole; SbS
F1 Arven
    Suppliers: Bree
Asmer Juno
Usually cuts into June, producing large heads of superb quality before the
first early summer cauliflowers are ready. (Mars)
    Suppliers: Mars
Asmer Pinnacle
Heads mid-late May with good quality heads for this difficult period. Hardy
and particularly useful in Midland and Northern areas. (Sutt)
    Suppliers: Dob; Sutt
Asmer Snowcap March
The earliest variety of the hardyEnglish type. (Mars)
    Suppliers: Mars
F1 Aston Purple
    Suppliers: Yate
Aubade
    Suppliers: Foth
Autumn Giant
Large heads for cutting from October onwards. (EWK)
    Suppliers: Barb; Chil; EWK; John; JWB; Mole; Rog; SbS; VanH
Autumn Giant 3
    Suppliers: CGar; SbS
Autumn Giant 4
    Suppliers: Dob; Sutt

Autumn Glory
An old favourite but still deservedly popular. Exceedingly large heads of the finest quality. (Unwi)
Suppliers: Unwi
F1 Aviso
Suppliers: Toze
F1 Baco
Suppliers: RSlu; Toze
F1 Balmoral
Suppliers: Yate
F1 Bambi
Suppliers: Bree
Barrier Reef
Compact habit, well-protected deep, white, solid curds. Matures late October. (Sutt)
Suppliers: Brwn; CGar; Chil; D&D; EWK; John; JWB; Mars; Mole; Rog; SbS; Sutt; Tuck; VanH; Yate
Batsman
A very vigorous variety which produces excellent quality white curds which are well protected. (Foth)
Suppliers: Foth; Toze
F1 Bergen
Suppliers: Bree
Briac 30
Australian type with large heads and short growing habit. Sow mid-May for maturity to mid-November. (EWK)
Suppliers: Toze; Yate
F1 Briten
Suppliers: Bree
F1 Calan
Suppliers: Toze
Canberra
Australian variety for November cutting. Large solid heads of excellent colour and quality. (EWK)
Suppliers: CGar; Mars; Rog; SbS; SMM
F1 Candid Charm
Suppliers: EWK; OGC; Rog; Suff; Tuck; Yate
Cargill
Suppliers: T&M; Yate
F1 Carlos
Suppliers: RSlu; Toze

F1 Castlegrant
Suppliers: Yate

F1 Ciren
Suppliers: Bree

Coolabah
From mid-May sowings high quality curds cuttable from mid-September through October. (CGar)
Suppliers: SbS

Cora 40
Suppliers: Yate

Corvilia
Large head size, rather smooth and slightly domed in shape. Late summer to late autumn. (EWK)
Suppliers: Yate

Decidura
Suppliers: Foth

Dok Elgon
Matures about 13 weeks after planting. Excellent as an early and late autumn crop. Vigorous growing with well-covered, firm, round, snow-white heads. (Mars)
Suppliers: Brwn; Cart; CGar; D&D; Dob; EWK; Foth; John; JWB; Mars; Mole; OGC; Rob; Rog; RSlu; SMM; Sutt; T&M; Toze; Tuck; Unwi; VanH

Dominant
Grows well in dry conditions with strong broad foliage for good protection. Autumn heading. (EWK)
Suppliers: Brwn; EWK; Mars; Mole; OGC

F1 Dova
Suppliers: Brwn; RSlu; Toze

F1 Elby
Suppliers: Dob; RSlu; T&M; Toze

English Winter
Suppliers: John; SbS

Ewk's Late June
Suppliers: JWB; SbS

Ewk's May Star
Suppliers: JWB

Fleurly
An excellent addition! Fleurly produces solid clear white heads of exceptionally high quality. Cut from mid-late April from a late-May sowing. (Dob)
    Suppliers: Dob; Mole
Flora Blanca
Matures September and October. Deep, pure white heads of first-class quality. Excellent for exhibition. (Sutt)
    Suppliers: Sutt
Florian 51
Exceptional solid white heads and a strong weather resistance. (Foth)
    Suppliers: Toze; Yate
Fortuna
    Suppliers: John; Mole
F1 Fremont
    Suppliers: RSlu
Garant
Quick growing mini cauliflower. (EWK)
    Suppliers: EWK; OGC; Suff
Grandessa
Medium large heads of pure white for autumn cutting. Strong mid green foliage giving excellent protection. (EWK)
    Suppliers: Bakk
Grodan
    Suppliers: Mole
F1 Hawkesbury
    Suppliers: Yate
Idol
    Suppliers: Dob
Inca
April heading variety with excellent white heads. Strong leaf protection and very frost resistant. (EWK)
    Suppliers: Barb; CGar; EWK; OGC; Rog; SbS; Suff; Toze
Jaudy 45
    Suppliers: Toze; Yate
F1 Jerome
    Suppliers: Mars
June Glory
    Suppliers: SbS
June Supreme
    Suppliers: SbS

Juno
Winter heading, excellent quality, sow April to June matures following May/June. (JWB)
   Suppliers: JWB
Jura
   Suppliers: SbS
King
Medium large heads of pure white for autumn cutting. Strong mid green foliage giving excellent protection. (EWK)
   Suppliers: EWK; Mole; Rog; SbS; Yate
Lateman
A versatile, medium sized variety with lovely deep white curds. Sow from March to May for cutting August to October. (Dob)
   Suppliers: Brwn; Dob; VanH
Lawnya
   Suppliers: SbS
Lecerf
   Suppliers: VanH
Linas
   Suppliers: SbS
Lincoln Early
   Suppliers: SbS
F1 Linday
   Suppliers: Bree
F1 Lindon
   Suppliers: Bree
F1 Linero
   Suppliers: Bree
F1 Linex
   Suppliers: Bree
F1 Linmont
   Suppliers: Bree
F1 Lintop
   Suppliers: Bree
Macerata
   Suppliers: Toze
Marchpast
   Suppliers: Bree; SbS

Markanta
Extra high quality, with pure white, deep curds produced from early May onwards. (Mars)
Suppliers: Foth; JWB; Mars; SbS; Unwi
F1 Marmalade
Suppliers: Yate
May Glory
Suppliers: SbS
Maya
Late May heading. Very hardy, produces well protected, high quality curds. Can be sown as late as June. (Tuck)
Suppliers: CGar; D&D; EWK; OGC; Rog; SbS; Tuck
Mechelse Carillon
Suppliers: Bree; SbS; Toze
Mechelse Classic
Suppliers: SbS
Mechelse Romax
Suppliers: SbS
Minaret
Suppliers: Yate
F1 Montano
Suppliers: Bree; Mars
F1 Nautilus
Suppliers: Brwn; Toze
Nevada
Suppliers: SbS
Orco
Suppliers: SbS
Oze
Suppliers: SbS
Pacific Charm
Suppliers: SbS
F1 Pamir
Suppliers: RSlu
Panda
Suppliers: D&D; EWK; Tuck
Perfection
A very reliable variety for October or January sowings. (Brwn)
Suppliers: Brwn; EWK; Mole; SbS; SMM; Toze; Yate

Pinacle
Suppliers: SbS
F1 Plana
Suppliers: Mars; RSlu; T&M
Predil
Suppliers: RSlu
Predominant
An easy to grow, mini-cauliflower, can be sown later for heads maturing in September-October. (T&M)
Suppliers: Toze
Primel No 25
Suppliers: Toze
Purple Cape
A hardy purple cauliflower cropping in February and March. The curd turns green when cooked and have a fine flavour. (Mars)
Suppliers: Bree; Chil; Dob; John; JWB; Mars; Mole; SbS; Suff; T&M; Unwi
Purple Oak
Suppliers: SbS
Purple Queen
Vigorous grower and very uniform. Deep purple heads for early autumn maturity. (EWK)
Suppliers: Barb; CGar; EWK; Rog; VanH
Revito
Suppliers: Bakk; SbS; Toze; Yate
Rosalind
A quick growing purple headed variety for autumn cutting. Sow late May and June. Well worth trying. (Suff)
Suppliers: Cart; Suff; Toze
Royal Oak
Very fine late variety, heads in May. (Barb)
Suppliers: Chil
F1 SG 4019
Suppliers: Bree
F1 SG 4055
Suppliers: Bree
F1 Sergeant
Suppliers: Bree
Sernio
Suppliers: RSlu

F1 Serrano
Suppliers: Bree
Sierra
Suppliers: Brwn; RSlu
Snow Crown
Snows winter white, sow May/June, January cutting. (Barb)
Suppliers: JWB; Mars; SbS; Unwi
F1 Snow Diana
Suppliers: SbS
F1 Snow February
Suppliers: SbS
F1 Snow Flake
Suppliers: Bakk
F1 Snow King
Suppliers: T&M
F1 Snow Prince
Suppliers: EWK; SbS
Snow White
Specially recommended for southern and western regions. Unsuitable for cold or exposed areas. Pure white solid curds, for use March-April. (Sutt)
Suppliers: Sutt
Snow's Winter White
Invaluable and popular mid-winter cauliflower. Cold tolerant and easier to grow than spring varieties. (T&M)
Suppliers: T&M
Snowball
Compact and very early with solid pure white heads of superb quality. Can be sown as early as January and also during autumn. (Dob)
Suppliers: Cart; CGar; Dob; EWK; Foth; John; JWB; Mole; Rog; SbS; SMM; Suff; Sutt; VanH
F1 Snowbred
This is a greatly improved type from the original, and is a first class early market variety, we continue to offer it because of the demand. (Brwn)
Suppliers: EWK; OGC   .
Snowcap
Very late variety that can be cut over a long period. Ready in 22 weeks from an early June sowing. (EWK)
Suppliers: Barb; CGar; D&D; EWK; JWB; Mole; OGC; Rog; SbS; Tuck; Yate
Snowy River
Suppliers: SbS

Solide
Suppliers: Mole
St George
A later variety, ready for harvesting in April and May, giving solid pure white heads. (John)
Suppliers: Chil; John; SbS
St Gwithian
Suppliers: SbS
St Keverne
Suppliers: SbS
St Mark
Suppliers: SbS
St Mawes
Suppliers: SbS
Starlight
Upright, leafy frame, suitable for cropping from early summer to early autumn. (EWK)
Suppliers: SbS
F1 Stella
Suppliers: Toze
Swan Lake
Suppliers: SbS
Tavia
Suppliers: Yate
F1 Taymount
Suppliers: Yate
Triskel 22
Produces superb quality heads in the hotter months of the year when other varieties are often poor. Sow April to mature late August; early May for September. (Mars)
Suppliers: Toze; Yate
F1 Tulchan
Suppliers: Sutt; Yate
Veitch's Self Protecting
Suppliers: Barb; CGar; D&D; EWK; Rog; SbS; T&M
Vernon
Suppliers: Mole
Vilna
The latest maturing overwinter cauliflower. Maturing end of May to mid-June. Very hardy. (Brwn)
Suppliers: Brwn; CGar; SbS; Toze

F1 Violet Queen
Suppliers: Bree; OGC; SbS; Sutt; Yate
Vision
Suppliers: SbS; Toze
F1 Walcheren SG 4043
Suppliers: Bree
F1 Walcheren SG 4044
Suppliers: Bree
Walcheren Winter
The first heads will be ready in early April but the plants continue to come into cut throughout April and May for a full six weeks. (Mars)
Suppliers: Dob; VanH
Walcheren Winter 1 Armado April
Suppliers: Barb; Brwn; CGar; D&D; JWB; Mars; Mole; OGC; Rog; RSlu; SbS; T&M; Toze; Tuck; VanH
Walcheren Winter 2 Armado May
Suppliers: Mole; RSlu; SbS; Toze
Walcheren Winter 3
Suppliers: Sutt
Walcheren Winter 3 Armado Tardo
Suppliers: Mole; RSlu; SbS; T&M; Toze
Walcheren Winter 5
Suppliers: SbS
Walcheren Winter 5 Maystar
Selected stock for the British climate. Solid pure white heads are well protected and ready in May. (OGC)
Suppliers: Bree; OGC; SbS; Toze; Yate
Walcheren Winter 6
Suppliers: SbS
Walcheren Winter 7
Suppliers: SbS
Wallaby
For heading late September-early October, this variety is outstanding for its top quality solid white curds. The well-protected heads are ideal for freezing. (Sutt)
Suppliers: JWB; Mole; OGC; SbS; SMM; Sutt; T&M; Toze; Yate
White Ball
Very white, deep curd with good covering leaves. May be autumn sown without going blind. A relatively new variety but already very popular. (Foth)
Suppliers: Foth

F1 White Dove
Suppliers: Toze; Yate
White Fox
Suppliers: Bree; JWB; SbS; Toze
White Pearl
Suppliers: Yate
White Rock
White Rock produces plenty of outer and inner leaves which protect the curd, it is very adaptable and is grown for the mild-July to October period. (Brwn)
Suppliers: Bree; Brwn; JWB; Mole; SbS; Toze
White Satin
Suppliers: Bree
White Summer
Produces firm, round heads of excellent quality for late summer and early autumn cutting. This variety has proved very reliable even under adverse weather conditions. (Unwi)
Suppliers: Bree
F1 Whitney
Suppliers: RSlu
F1 Woomera
Suppliers: Toze; Yate
F1 Yann 37
Suppliers: Toze
F1 Zara
Suppliers: Toze

Synonyms

All Seasons see All The Year Round
Angers Early see Angers No 2
Angers Extra Early see Angers No 1
Angers Extra Late see Angers No 5
Angers Half Early see Angers No 3
Angers Late see Angers No 4
Asmer Bostonian see Walcheren Winter 5
Dutch May Heading 0581 see Walcheren Winter 5
Early Feltham see Angers No 2
Erfurt Prima see Snowball
Extra Early Feltham see Angers No 1
Extra Late Feltham see Angers No 5
Herfstreuzen see Autumn Giant
Late Adonis see Walcheren Winter 7

Late Feltham see Angers No 4
Majestic see Autumn Giant 3
Mechelse Lincoln Early see Lincoln Early
New Late Dutch see Walcheren Winter 6
Polaris see Alpha
Snow Cap see Snowcap
Thanet see Walcheren Winter 3
Walcheren Winter Aprilex see Aprilex
Walcheren Winter Armado April see Armado April
Walcheren Winter Armado May see Armado May
Walcheren Winter Armado Quick see Armado Quick
Walcheren Winter Armado Tardo see Armado Tardo
Walcheren Winter Arminda see Arminda
Walcheren Winter Marchpast see Marchpast
Walcheren Winter Markanta see Markanta
Walcheren Winter Maya see Maya
Westmarsh Early see Angers No 2
Yopal see Zara

Celeriac

Apium graveolens

Botanically identical to celery, but grown for the swollen roots rather than for the leaf stalks.

Alabaster
Suppliers: John; SbS
Balder
Suppliers: Brwn; Chil; OGC; SbS
Brilliant
Suppliers: Dob
Correcta
Suppliers: Bakk
Giant Prague
Suppliers: Bakk; Barb; CGar; D&D; EWK; JWB; Mole; Rog; SbS; Tuck; VanH
Iram
Suppliers: Unwi
Marble Ball
Suppliers: Butc; Foth; SbS; SMM; Suff
Monarch
Suppliers: Bree; T&M; Toze; Yate

Nemona
    Suppliers: SbS
Snow White
    Suppliers: Mars
Tellus
    Suppliers: Sutt
Synonyms
    Albaster see Alabaster
    Boule de Marbre see Marble Ball

Celery

Autumn Gold
    Suppliers: Foth; SbS
Avonpearl
    Suppliers: Barb; Butc; CGar; OGC; Rog; SbS; Suff
Brydon's Prize White
    Suppliers: JWB
Celebrity
    Suppliers: Brwn; Dob; Mars; Mole; SbS; Yate
Cutting Celery
    Suppliers: Suff
Galaxy
    Suppliers: T&M
Giant Pink
    Suppliers: Brwn; Butc; Dob; JWB; SbS; Suff; Sutt
Giant Red
    Suppliers: Butc; CGar; Chil; Mars; Mole; SbS; Sutt; Yate
Giant Solid White
    Suppliers: Mole
Giant White
    Suppliers: Brwn; Chil; D&D; Dob; EWK; Rog; SbS; Tuck; VanH
Golden Self Blanching 3
    Suppliers: Bakk; Barb; cART; CGar; Chil; D&D; Dob; EWK; John;
    JWB; Mole; OGC; Rog; SbS; Sutt; Tuck; VanH
Golden Spartan
    Suppliers: SbS
Green Sleeves
    Suppliers: Dob; T&M; Yate
Green Utah
    Suppliers: EWK; JWB; OGC

Greenlet
Suppliers: RSlu
Greensnap
Suppliers: Butc; Rog; SbS
Harvest Moon
Suppliers: SbS
Hopkins Fenlander
Suppliers: Mars; SbS; T&M; Toze
Ideal
Suppliers: Butc
Ivory Tower
Suppliers: Foth; Sutt
Lathom Self Blanching
Suppliers: Bree; Mole; SbS; Toze; Unwi
Loret
Suppliers: RSlu; Yate
Mammoth Pink
Suppliers: CGar; Rob
Mammoth White
Suppliers: CGar; Rob
Martine
Suppliers: CGar; Rob
Navajo
Suppliers: Bree
Pearly Queen
Suppliers: SbS
Selfire
Suppliers: SbS
Sioux
Suppliers: Bree
Solid Pink
Suppliers: OGC
Solid White
Suppliers: OGC; Sutt
Soup Celery d'Amsterdam
Suppliers: Bakk
Stardust
Suppliers: SbS
Triumph
Suppliers: John; Sutt

Utah 52-70
Suppliers: Bakk; RSlu; SbS; Toze
F1 Victoria
Suppliers: Toze
White Pascal
Suppliers: John; SbS
Wright's Giant White
Suppliers: Barb
Synonyms
American Green see Greensnap
Brydon's Prize Red see Giant Red
Chatteris see Lathom Self Blanching
Clayworth Pink see Giant Pink
Clayworth Prize Pink see Giant Pink
Fenlander see Hopkins Fenlander
Golden Self Blanching see Golden Self Blanching 3
Green see Greensnap
Groene Pascal see White Pascal
Jason Self Blanching see Lathom Self Blanching
Mammoth Pink see Giant Pink
Red Claret see Tall Utah 52/70
Unrivalled Pink see Giant Pink
Utah 52-70 see Tall Utah 52/70

Chenopodium berlandieri
Chenopodium berlandieri
Huauzontli
A Mexican annual cultivated for its mild flavoured leaves which are traditionally eaten fried with onions or in salads when they are young. They produce large quantities of seeds which can be ground to make flour for tortillas or as a millet substitute and it has been suggested as a potential new grain crop. Cold weather turns the leaves red. (Futu)
Suppliers: Futu

Chenopodium foliosum
Chenopodium foliosum
Beetberry
An annual similar to Fat Hen which bears numerous red fruits somewhat similar to mulberries in the leaf axils. The flavour is not great, but they are sweet and attractive and can be used mixed with other fruits in pies, fruit salads &c. A fun plant, popular with children and unusual in that it is one of the few berry-bearing members of the family. Vigorous plants which self-seed easily and are thus suited to low-maintenance gardening. (Futu)
    Suppliers: Futu

Chicory
Cichorium intybus
Two sorts are grown, the forcing, sugarloaf types and the heading types, often called radicchio
    Apollo
        Suppliers: Mars
    Canasta
        Suppliers: Bree
    Crispa
        Suppliers: Butc
    Crystal Head
        Suppliers: Bakk; Foth; Unwi
    F1 Flash
        Suppliers: Bakk; T&M
    Gradina
        Suppliers: SbS
    Mechelse Medium-early
        Suppliers: Bakk
    Robin
        Suppliers: Bree
    Snowflake
        Suppliers: Dob; T&M
    Sugar Loaf
        Suppliers: Butc; D&D; EWK; JWB; OGC; Rog; SbS; SMM; Suff; Sutt; Tuck; VanH
    Videna
        Suppliers: Bakk

Witloof
Suppliers: Bakk; Barb; Butc; CGar; Chil; D&D; EWK; John; JWB; Mole; OGC; Rog; SbS; Suff; Sutt; Tuck
F1 Zoom
Suppliers: Bree; Dob; Suff
Synonyms
Brussels Witloof see Witloof
Pain de Sucre see Sugar Loaf
Pan di Zucchero see Sugar Loaf
Winter Fare see Snowflake

Chicory Radicchio
Cichoirum intybus
Alouette
Suppliers: Foth; T&M
Bianca di Milano
Suppliers: Suff
Biondissima di Trieste
Suppliers: Suff
Cesare
Suppliers: John; Suff
Giulio
Suppliers: Suff
Grumolo Verde
Suppliers: Suff
F1 Jupiter
Suppliers: Toze
Magdeburg
Suppliers: SbS; Suff
Marsica
Suppliers: Bree
F1 Medusa
Suppliers: Bakk; Toze; Yate
Palla Rossa
Suppliers: EWK
Palla rossa Zorzi precoce
Suppliers: Barb; Butc; Cart; D&D; JWB; Mars; Rog; SbS; Sutt; Tuck; Unwi
Poncho
Suppliers: John

Prima Rossa
  Suppliers: Yate
Prima Rossa Special
  Suppliers: Yate
Red devil
  Suppliers: Dob
Rossa di Treviso
  Suppliers: Bakk; OGC; Suff
Rossa di Verona
  Suppliers: Bakk; OGC; SbS; Suff
Scarpia
  Suppliers: Bakk
Variegata di Castelfranco
  Suppliers: Suff
Variegata di Chioggia
  Suppliers: Suff
Synonyms
  Chioggia see Alouette
  Red Treviso see Rossa di Treviso
  Red Verona see Rossa di Verona

Chinese Artichoke
Stachys affinis
Slightly fiddlier than Jerusalem artichokes (to which they are not related) but with a flavour altogether more delicate. Joy Larkcom says they are slightly nutty and reminiscent of globe artichokes, new potatoes and water chestnuts.
Chinese Artichoke
A hardy perennial tuber crop with hairy leaves and purplish flowers, which produces large numbers of small, white, maggot-shaped tubers with a crunchy texture that are excellent raw in salads, cooked in stir-fries, soups and stews, or pickled in vinegar. They can be harvested after the foliage dies down and are best stored damp or left in the ground until required. The plants are vigorous and will regrow from any tubers left in the ground making them an ideal low maintenance crop. (Futu)
  Suppliers: Futu; Poyn
Crosnes
  Suppliers: Bakk

Chinese Broccoli

Brassica oleracea var. *alboglabra*

Also known as Chinese kale, Gai Lan and Kailan are the Mandarin and Cantonese names for this vegetable, rather than varieties in their own right. Very accomodating in its climatic requirements.

F1 Green Lance
Suppliers: CGar; Chil; D&D; EWK; OGC; SbS; SMM
Kailan
Not a variety name.
Suppliers: SbS; SMM; Suff
Kintsai
Suppliers: CGar; D&D; EWK; SbS; SMM

Chinese Chives

Allium tuberosus

Chinese leek and garlic chives are other common names for this vegetable, almost all parts of which are used.

Broadleaf
Suppliers: Chil; D&D; EWK; T&M
Chinese Chives
Suppliers: Dob; SMM

Choy Sum

Flowering brassicas, of many species.

All are brassicas, grown for their flowers. Joy Larkcom divides them into six different groups. Choy Sum, or Pak Tsoi Sum, is flowering white cabbage. Hong Tsoi Sum, or Hon Tsai tai, is purple flowered choy sum. Flowering Pak Choi is a variety of Pak Choi grown for its flowers. Edible Oil Seed Rapes are not the rapes grown in the west, but are a source of oil for lamps and cooking, and leaves and buds for eating. Hybrid Flowering Rapes are a new development from Japan, which Joy Larkcom says are the best members of the tribe for the gardener. And Brocoletto types are similar to the broccoli raab grown in southern Europe.

F1 Bouquet
Suppliers: CGar; D&D; EWK; SMM

Choy Sum (Purple Flowered)
    Suppliers: OGC; SMM
Hon Tsai Tai
Not a true variety name.
    Suppliers: Bakk; Chil; Suff

Chrysanthemum Greens
Chrysanthemum coronarium
Shungiku is the Japanese name for these members of the daisy family, which are also known as Chop Suey Greens and Japanese Greens. There are two basic types, those with small, serrated leaves and those with larger, broader leaves.
    Shungiku
    Shungiku is the Japanese name for Chrysanthemum Greens in general, not a single variety.
        Suppliers: CGar; Chil; D&D; Dob; EWK; Futu; OGC; SbS; SMM; Suff

Corn Salad
Valerianella locusta
Also known as Lamb's Lettuce, it is a useful salad crop for the winter months.
    Cavallo
        Suppliers: T&M
    Corn Salad
        Suppliers: Butc; CGar; Cham; D&D; EWK; Foth; Futu; John; Mole; Poyn; SMM; Tuck
    Grote Noordhollandse
        Suppliers: Bakk; Bree; Chil; Dob; JWB; OGC; SbS; Suff; Sutt; Unwi
    Jade
        Suppliers: Mars
    Louviers
        Suppliers: Bakk
    Verte de Cambrai
        Suppliers: Suff
    Vit
        Suppliers: Suff
    Volhart
        Suppliers: Bakk

Synonyms
    D'Olanda see Grote Noordhollandse

Cress
Many species
Various species, including salad rape and mustard, are also known and sold as cress.
    American Land
        Suppliers: Bakk; Butc; CGar; Cham; Cham; Chil; D&D; Dob; EWK; Futu; John; JWB; Mars; OGC; Poyn; Rog; SbS; SMM; Suff; Sutt; T&M; Tuck; Unwi; VanH
    Armada
        Suppliers: Mars
    Curled
        Suppliers: CGar; Chil; D&D; John; Mars; Rog; Sutt
    Double Curled
        Suppliers: Butc
    Extra Curled
        Suppliers: T&M
    Extra Double Curled
        Suppliers: Dob
    Extra Fine Curled
        Suppliers: Barb
    Fine Curled
        Suppliers: Cart; EWK; Foth; SbS; Suff; Unwi; Yate
    Greek
        Suppliers: Suff
    Large Leaved
        Suppliers: Bakk; Brwn
    Plain
        Suppliers: Bakk; CGar; EWK; JWB; Mole; Rog; SbS; VanH
    Reform
        Suppliers: SbS
    Super Salad
        Suppliers: Dob

Cucumber
Cucumis sativus
Generally divided in to ridge, or outdoor, and frame, or indoor, types. Gherkins are smaller, and may be grown either indoors or outdoors.

F1 Anka
Suppliers: Bakk
F1 Aramon
Suppliers: John
F1 Avanti
Suppliers: Yate
F1 Bronco
Suppliers: Yate
F1 Brunex
Suppliers: OGC; Yate
Chinese Long Green
Suppliers: Bakk
F1 Cordoba
Suppliers: EWK
F1 Crispy Salad
Suppliers: T&M
F1 Daleva
Suppliers: Yate
F1 Danimas
Suppliers: Dob; Yate
Delicatesse
Suppliers: Bakk
F1 Farbiola
Suppliers: Toze
Hoffmans Giganta
Suppliers: Bakk
F1 Janeen
Suppliers: Yate
Mammoth
Suppliers: T&M
Marketmore
Suppliers: Toze
F1 Mustang
Suppliers: Yate

F1 **Slice King**
  Suppliers: D&D; EWK; OGC
F1 **Sweet Success**
  Suppliers: Bakk
F1 **Uniflora**
  Suppliers: CGar; EWK; Rog; SMM; VanH
Synonyms
  Delikatess see Delicatesse

Cucumber Frame
F1 **Aidas**
  Suppliers: T&M
F1 **Aramon**
  Suppliers: Mole
F1 **Athene**
  Suppliers: Mars
F1 **Best Seller**
  Suppliers: John
F1 **Birgit**
  Suppliers: Bakk; Brwn; Dob; Foth; John; Mole; Toze; Yate
F1 **Brunex**
  Suppliers: Mole
F1 **Carmen**
  Suppliers: Mole; T&M
Conqueror
  Suppliers: Dob; OGC
Diana
  Suppliers: Unwi
F1 **Euphya**
  Suppliers: Mole
F1 **Fembaby**
  Suppliers: T&M
F1 **Femdam**
  Suppliers: Barb; Brwn; Butc; CGar; EWK; Rog; SMM
F1 **Femspot**
  Suppliers: Foth; Mole; Sutt; Tuck
F1 **Fenumex**
  Suppliers: Barb; CGar; D&D; EWK; OGC; Rog; Suff; Tuck
F1 **Kamaron**
  Suppliers: Mole

King George
   Suppliers: CGar; Rob
F1 Landora
   Suppliers: Sutt
F1 Monique
   Suppliers: Mole
F1 Pepinex '69
   Suppliers: Barb; Bree; Brwn; Butc; Cart; CGar; Dob; EWK; John; JWB;
   Mars; Rog; Unwi
F1 Petita
   Suppliers: Brwn; Butc; CGar; D&D; Dob; EWK; Foth; John; Mole;
   OGC; Rog; SMM; Sutt; Toze; Unwi
Sigmadew
   Suppliers: Sutt
F1 Superator
   Suppliers: Brwn; Mole
F1 Sweet Alphee
   Suppliers: Suff
Telegraph
   Suppliers: Cart; CGar; Dob; EWK; John; JWB; Mars; OGC; Sutt; Toze;
   Unwi; Yate
Telegraph Improved
   Suppliers: Barb; Brwn; D&D; Foth; Mole; Rog; Suff; Sutt; Tuck; VanH
F1 Tyria
   Suppliers: Brwn; Mars
Synonyms
   Rollison's Telegraph see Telegraph Improved

Cucumber Gherkin
F1 Accordia
   Suppliers: Mole
F1 Arena
   Suppliers: John
Beit Alpha Ellam
   Suppliers: SbS
F1 Bestal
   Suppliers: Mars
Boston Green
   Suppliers: SbS

F1 Conda
Suppliers: Unwi
F1 Dex
Suppliers: Bakk
F1 Fanfare
Suppliers: Foth
Gherkin
Suppliers: Barb; CGar; D&D; EWK; Rog
Hokus
Suppliers: Bakk; Dob; SbS
F1 Liberty
Suppliers: T&M
National
Suppliers: OGC; SbS
Parisian Pickling
Suppliers: Bakk; SbS
Pointsett
Suppliers: SbS
Sena
Suppliers: Brwn
Tera
Suppliers: SbS
Toret
Suppliers: SbS
Venlo Pickling
Suppliers: Bakk; Butc; JWB; SbS; Sutt
Synonyms
De Vorgebirg see Venlo
De Vorgebirg see Venlo Pickling
Vert Petit de Paris see Parisian Pickling

Cucumber Ridge
Apple Shaped
Suppliers: JWB
F1 Burpee Hybrid
Suppliers: Dob
F1 Burpless Tasty Green
Suppliers: Barb; Butc; CGar; D&D; EWK; Foth; JWB; Mars; Mole; OGC; Rog; SbS; Suff; Sutt; T&M; Tuck

F1 Bush Champion
  Suppliers: Cart; Dob; John; Sutt; T&M
Bush Crop
  Suppliers: Bakk; Foth; Mars
Crystal Apple
  Suppliers: Butc; CGar; EWK; Mole; OGC; Rog; SbS; Suff; Sutt; VanH
King of the Ridge
  Suppliers: JWB
Kyoto
  Suppliers: Barb; CGar; D&D; EWK; Rog; SbS; Suff; T&M
Long Green Ridge
  Suppliers: Barb; CGar; Chil; EWK; John; Rog; SbS; SMM; Sutt; Yate
Marketer
  Suppliers: SbS
Marketmore
  Suppliers: Mars
Masterpiece
  Suppliers: Barb; EWK; OGC; Rog; SbS; VanH
Perfection
  Suppliers: Brwn; Foth; Mole; SbS
F1 Tokyo Slicer
  Suppliers: Toze; Unwi
Yamato
  Suppliers: Butc; CGar; EWK; OGC; SMM
Synonyms
  Bedfordshire Prize see Long Green Ridge
  Burpless see Burpless Tasty Green
  Long Prickly see Long Green Ridge
  Marketeer see Marketer
  Stockwood see Long Green Ridge

Dandelion
Taraxacum officinalis
The leaves, green or blanched, have long been used in salads.
  A Coeur Plein
    Suppliers: Suff
  Broad Leaved
    Suppliers: JWB
  Dandelion
    Suppliers: Sutt

Salad Dandelion
Suppliers: CGar; Cham; D&D
Thick-leaved
Suppliers: Chil

Earth Chestnut
Bunium bulbocastaneum
Earth Chestnut
A vigorous perennial producing small tuberous roots said to taste like chestnuts when boiled. Seeds can be used as a condiment. A rare British native of chalk grasslands. (Futu)
Suppliers: Futu

Endive
Cichorium endivia
Related to chicory, but forming a lettuce-like head similar to radicchio chicory.
Avant Garde Winter
Suppliers: Bakk
Casco d'Oro
Suppliers: Bakk
Coquette
Suppliers: T&M
Cornet De Bordeaux
Suppliers: Suff
De Ruffec
Suppliers: Foth; SbS
Dolly
Suppliers: Mole; SbS
Elodie
Suppliers: Bree
Elysee
Suppliers: Yate
Eminence
Suppliers: Brwn
Fine Maraichere
Suppliers: Suff
Glory
Suppliers: Yate

Green Curled
 Suppliers: Barb; Bree; Butc; Chil; D&D; EWK; John; JWB; OGC; Rog;
 SbS; Sutt; Toze; Tuck; Unwi; VanH
Ione
 Suppliers: Dob; Toze
Jeti
 Suppliers: SMM
Markant
 Suppliers: Brwn
Minerva
 Suppliers: Yate
No. 5 2
 Suppliers: Bakk; Butc; Dob; JWB; OGC; SbS; Sutt
No. 5 Malan
 Suppliers: RSlu
No. 5 Sinco
 Suppliers: Bree
President
 Suppliers: Bakk
Riccia Pancalieri
 Suppliers: OGC; Suff
Sally
 Suppliers: Cart; Mars; Mole; SbS; Yate
Sanda
 Suppliers: Bree
Scarola Verde
 Suppliers: Suff
St Laurent-Midori
 Suppliers: Bakk
Tres Fine Maraichere Coquette
 Suppliers: RSlu
Wallonne
 Suppliers: RSlu; Suff
White Curled
 Suppliers: Bakk
Synonyms
 Batavian Broad Leaved see No. 5 2
 Batavian Green see No. 5 2
 Breedblad Volhart Winter see Avant Garde Winter
 De Ruffec see Ruffec

Fijne Krul Groen see Green Curled
Moss Curled see Green Curled

Fennel

Foeniculum vulgare var. *azoricum*

Florence Fennel, grown for the swollen stem bases, rather than the herb fennel.

Bronze
Suppliers: Poyn
Cantino
Suppliers: Mars; SMM; Suff; Yate
Di Firenze
Suppliers: Butc; CGar; Chil; D&D; EWK; OGC
Fino
Suppliers: Bakk; Bree; Dob; Foth; Mole; Poyn; Toze; Unwi; Yate
Green
Suppliers: Poyn
Herald
Suppliers: T&M
Perfection
Suppliers: Suff; Tuck
Sirio
Suppliers: Sutt
Tardo
Suppliers: Bree; Toze
Synonyms
Florence see Di Firenze
Sweet Florence see Di Firenze
Zefa Fino see Fino
Zefa Tardo see Tardo

French Bean Climbing

Phaseolus vulgaris

Blue Lake White Seeded
Requires sticks or a climbing frame. Very productive and suitable for freezing with an excellent flavour. Pods can also be dried for use as haricot. (OGC)
Suppliers: Barb; Bree; Brwn; Chil; D&D; Dob; EWK; Foth; John; JWB; Mole; OGC; Rog; SMM; Suff; Sutt; Tuck; VanH

Borlotto
Unusual and attractive, the 6in. flat and broad pods are pale green with red stripes. When young the pods are cut and eaten as a normal french bean, left they may be shelled and the seeds eaten. (Foth)
   Suppliers: Foth
Borlotto Lingua di Fuoco
This is the original Fire Tongue strain from Italy. May be eaten as green pods but grown mainly for delicious semi-dry beans and dry beans. Spectacular green pods with red stripes make this very decorative. (Suff)
   Suppliers: Suff
Corona d'Oro
A climbing bean giving heavy yields of golden-yellow pods, round in section and succulent and tender in texture. Regular picking will encourage further pod formation of this useful and decorative variety. (John)
   Suppliers: EWK; John; Rog
Cristal
   Suppliers: Yate
Glastada
   Suppliers: RSlu
Goldmarie
   Suppliers: Sutt
Helda
   Suppliers: Bakk; RSlu; Toze
Hunter
Flat podded variety. Yields heavy crops of long straight, stringless pods. (Foth)
   Suppliers: Barb; Brwn; D&D; EWK; Foth; John; Mars; OGC; Rog; Sutt; Tuck; VanH
Kentucky Blue
Excellent flavour and yields. Pods smooth and fleshy 16-17cm. (Bree)
   Suppliers: Bree; T&M
Kronos
   Suppliers: Mole
Kwintus
Despite the seed bulges which tend to be produced, the 9-11in. pods are tender, have a delicious distinctive flavour, and are usually stringless. (Dob)
   Suppliers: Dob; Mole
Largo
A smashing variety growing tall like a runner bean but producing round, stringless delicious pods. (Foth)
   Suppliers: Foth; Mars; Unwi

Limka
Suppliers: Yate

Mechelse Markt
Very much recommended to those who like a bean that is not too fleshy. Mechelse Markt produces clusters of so-called single beans which are unequalled as regards their fine flavour. Exceptionally heavy-cropping variety. (Bakk)
Suppliers: Bakk

Musica
Wide, flat, stringless pods with a delicious true beany flavour. Sown early it crops weeks before outdoor crops. Can also be sown outdoors. (T&M)
Suppliers: Mole; T&M

Neckarkoenigin
A long thick bean which can be used for slicing as well as for breaking. It will give a high yield per plant. Very resistant to diseases. (Bakk)
Suppliers: Bakk

Or du Rhin
A very fine old variety with broad flat yellow pods. Delicious picked young and cooked whole, also used in minestrone and for fresh shelling beans. The crispest and tastiest bean we have tried. Black seeded. A late maincrop. (Suff)
Suppliers: Bakk; Suff

Pea Bean
A climbing French bean. The flat poods should be harvested young to eat whole, or shelled out like peas. Alternatively leave to dry. Attractive bi-coloured seed. (OGC)
Suppliers: OGC; SbS

Purple Podded Climbing
Decorative and delicious, ht. approx. 150cm. (5ft). (Sutt)
Suppliers: CGar; Rog; Sutt

Rakker
Unquestionably the highest yielding variety producing record crops! Early and extremely prolific. Thick, fleshy beans with a delicious flavour. Rakker is also suitable for cultivation in a greenhouse. (Bakk)
Suppliers: Bakk

Rentmeester
A marked improvement of the old type Veense: very prolific, stringless, and with long, broad pods. Those who like a tender French bean for slicing with an outstanding flavour should not fail to try this variety. (Bakk)
Suppliers: Bakk

Robroy
A new climbing French bean, cream splashed with red. Very tender when cooked young. Good flavour and very attractive to grow. (CGar)
Suppliers: CGar; Rob

Robsplash
New climbing French bean, cream splashed purple, very tender when cooked young. (CGar)
Suppliers: CGar; Rob

Romano
Long, fleshy, tender, meaty and stringless pods, liberally loaded with flavour. (T&M)
Suppliers: T&M

Selka
Suppliers: Unwi

Serbo
Suppliers: Bree

Viola Cornetti
Typical Italian climbing bean with fine stringless purple podded beans. (OGC)
Suppliers: OGC; Suff

Violet Podded Stringless
Suppliers: Bakk; Foth

Wachs Goldstrahl
A long, thick-fleshed bean which produces a high yield of beautiful, golden-yellow pods. First class selection. (Bakk)
Suppliers: Bakk

Westlandia
A very richly bearing variety, producing beans in clusters of 4 to 6. The tasty beans are long and beautifully shaped. They have a dark green colour. An excellent, healthy vegetable. (Bakk)
Suppliers: Bakk

Synonyms
Blue Lake see Blue Lake White Seeded
Marvel of Venice see Or du Rhin
Meraviglia di Venezia see Or du Rhin
Purple Podded see Purple Podded Climbing
Rheingold see Or du Rhin

French Bean Dwarf

Acapulco
Suppliers: RSlu

Admires
Excellent dwarf French bean (large podded) for slicing. Early and very prolific. Admires is very much in demand, especially because of its resistance to many diseases. A variety with a very fine flavour. (Bakk)
Suppliers: Bakk

Allure
Dark green pod, long and slender; very productive. Resistant to most occurring bean diseases. (Bakk)
Suppliers: Bakk

Annabel
Stringless, flavoursome, slim pods 4-5in. in length borne in profusion. This compact item is ideal for the smaller garden and may also be grown in growing bags on the patio. (Dob)
Suppliers: CGar; Dob; EWK; Rog; Tuck

Aramis
Combines the high quality and flavour of the French 'filet' types, with the high yield and concentrated podset of modern Breeding. Very fine, round, stringless pods 14-15cm. in length. Pods are medium green colour with purple markings which disappear on cooking. (Bree)
Suppliers: Bree; Unwi

Bafin
This is like a true French haricot vert but stringless. It produces pencil slim, short beans ideal for freezing. (OGC)
Suppliers: OGC; Rog

Black Prince
Suppliers: SbS

Brown Dutch
One of the best drying beans. Floury texture and an excellent flavour. Easy to grow, and easy to shell. (Suff)
Suppliers: Bakk; OGC; Rog; Suff

Bush Blue Coco
A dwarf bean, remarkable for its dark colour. The stems are dark purple, the leaves tinged violet and the pods so dark as to be almost black. They do, however, turn green on cooking. A vigorous early maturing variety giving an abundance of pods.(John)
Suppliers: John

Bush Blue Lake
Suppliers: Rog
Canadian Wonder
Old established variety, producing very heavy crops of flat shaped pods. (EWK)
Suppliers: Barb; Barb; CGar; D&D; EWK; John; JWB; MAS; OGC; Rog; SbS
Cascade
Suppliers: Mole; Rog
Chevrier Vert
The classic French Flageolet dating from 1880. Tasty and tender greeny white fresh beans for classic French dishes. (Suff)
Suppliers: Bakk; Suff
Chinese Yellow
Drying bean. It is extremely resistant to less favourable weather conditions. Gives a heavy crop of yellow beans which turn white when cooking. (Bakk)
Suppliers: Bakk
Clyde
'Fine' whole bean, with good vigour and slightly early. Suitable for fresh market. (Bree)
Suppliers: Bree
Contender
Very early and productive. Useful for both the private gardener and the commercial grower. Can also be used as a haricot. (OGC)
Suppliers: Bakk; MAS; OGC; Rog; SbS
Cropper Teepee
As Purple, except the round pods are slightly larger, and medium green and white seeded. An excellent variety with disease resistance. (Foth)
Suppliers: Foth; John; Rog
Daisy
The long, stringless beans are held above the leaves so they are very easy to pick and are not splashed by soil. Excellent for freezing. (Mars)
Suppliers: Mars; T&M
Delinel
Ultra-fine deep green beans, with a unique texture and true French flavour. Heavy-cropping, it is one of the first of its type that is perfectly stringless. (Mars)
Suppliers: Mars

Deuil Fin Precoce
Compact plants ideal for cloche work, produce a good crop of steely grey-green pods with unique delicacy of flavour. (OGC)
Suppliers: OGC; Rog

Dutch Princess
Suppliers: VanH

Earlybird
A golden yellow podded variety which produces straight, fleshy pods, 6in. in length. Wax or yellow podded varieties are gaining in popularity, not only for their novelty value but also because of their excellent flavour and succulent texture. (John)
Suppliers: John; Rog

Echo
Stringless variety with pods turning yellow at maturity. Resistant to CBMV. A medium size pod for general purpose. (Bree)
Suppliers: Bree

Erato
Medium early, yellow-fleshed dwarf French bean, resistant to fairly bad weather conditions and, therefore, a sure cropper. Good-yielding variety. (Bakk)
Suppliers: Bakk

Fin de Bagnol
Suppliers: Foth; Suff

Forum
Suppliers: Bree; T&M

Golden Rocky
Suppliers: Rog

Golden Sands
Long pods which crop over a long period. Very good flavour. (EWK)
Suppliers: CGar; EWK; OGC; Tuck; VanH

Gresham
Suppliers: Mole; Rog

Harvester
Good for freezing or for dry haricot beans. (Barb)
Suppliers: JWB; Rog

Horsehead
From the breeder of the first 'socially acceptable' baked bean, this variety was tested by HDRA members some time ago and found to be particularly suitable for growing in the U.K. The dark red bean seeds are excellent for inclusion in soups, casserels and chile con carne. Taken young the pods can be eaten like conventional French beans. (OGC)
Suppliers: OGC

Keygold
Suppliers: Bakk

Kinghorn Wax
Medium-size. stringless, round, yellow wax beans with a fine flavour. (Foth)
Suppliers: Sutt

Larma
Very long-podded bean, 20-25cm! A richly bearing variety, highly resistant to diseases. (Bakk)
Suppliers: Bakk

Lasso
Suppliers: Foth

Laura
Suppliers: Toze; Yate

Limelight
Earliest bush bean. Exceptionally thick, fleshy fibreless and broad pods with a distinctive sweet flavour. Can be sown mid-summer for a heavy autumn crop. Also the shelled beans are delicious fresh or dried. (T&M)
Suppliers: T&M

Loch Ness
Suppliers: SbS; VanH

Masai
Suppliers: T&M

Masterpiece
Early, heavy cropping and suitable for forcing or growing outdoors. (Dob)
Suppliers: Barb; CGar; Dob; EWK; John; JWB; Mole; Rog; SbS; Sutt

Masterpiece Stringless
An improved, stringless development of Masterpiece for slicing. Very early. (Mars)
Suppliers: Cart; Mars; T&M; Unwi

Maxidor
A marked improvement on the old yellow-fleshed varieties. Very rich-bearing dwarf French bean. Healthy variety. An excellent addition to the existing range. (Bakk)
Suppliers: Bakk

Mirage
Produces long, fine-seeded dark green beans. This delicious dwarf French bean is extremely disease-resistant. A guaranteed sure cropper. (Bakk)
Suppliers: Bakk

Mont d'Or
Probably the finest flavoured golden wax with stringless flat pods. A very old French variety. Seed black. (Suff)
Suppliers: JWB; Mars; Mole; OGC; Rog; Suff

Montano
Suppliers: Bakk; John; Rog; Yate

Narbonne
Suppliers: RSlu

Nassau
A flat podded French bean of the romano type. The pods are stringless and of very high quality with better flavour than most snap beans. (OGC)
Suppliers: Brwn; John; OGC; Rog; Sutt; Yate

Nerina
A unique and very special variety with very slim and stringless, well flavoured non-fading dark green pods which stay smooth longer and freeze well. Erect habit for easy picking and resistant to CBMV. (T&M)
Suppliers: Rog; RSlu; T&M

Odessa
A very high yielding modern small podded variety ideal for the home gardener and for freezing and cooking whole. The pods are bright green in colour, rounded in section and have a maximum length of 5in. Pod quality is excellent with slow seed development, the flavour is superb. (John)
Suppliers: Bakk; John; Rog

Othello
An extremely fine-podded bean, also called 'faux-filet'. Othello is a needle bean, approx. 12cm. in length and with a cross-section of only approx 4-6mm. when picked young. First-class bean for gourmets. An impressive cropper. (Bakk)
Suppliers: Bakk

Processor
White seeded variety which can be used as a haricot bean when dried. (EWK)
Suppliers: Mole; Rog

Pros
Excellent when picked regularly and eaten fresh, but also bred with the freezer in mind. Each plant bears quantities of round, sweet, juicy round pods about 4-5in. long. When the first pods reach this size and can still be cleanly

snapped between the fingers, the whole plant can be lifted, the beans removed and frozen whole, not sliced or chopped. (Dob)

Suppliers: Dob; Mars; Unwi

Provider

Suppliers: Rog; Suff

Purple King

Suppliers: EWK; Rog

Purple Queen

One of the best flavours. A heavy yielder of glossy purple stringless beans. The round pods cook to an appetising dark green. (Foth)

Suppliers: Bakk; Foth; Rog; SMM; Sutt; Unwi

Purple Teepee

Fine flavoured, stringless pods are held high, for easy picking, turning rich green in boiling water. Very productive, quick to mature making it suitable for late, catching up sowings. (T&M)

Suppliers: Foth; Suff; T&M

Radar

A new, slim podded variety of the type favoured by gourmet restaurants because the young pods are tender, full of flavour and quite stringless. A multipodded type which can be picked in bunches at the 4in. stage and cooked without slicing. (T&M)

Suppliers: T&M

Record

A fairly early double dwarf French bean which will tolerate some cold. Well-known variety, still very much in demand. (Bakk)

Suppliers: Bakk

Regina

Drying bean. A vigorous grower, clearly recognizable by the red-coloured pods. The dried beans are decoratively spotted in red and have a marbled appreance. (Bakk)

Suppliers: Bakk

Rocquencourt

Suppliers: Suff

Roma II

One of the most widely grown beans in the business. Medium large fleshy pods that are traditionally cut in USA and Europe but can be served sliced or whole. (Bree)

Suppliers: Bree

Royalty

Suppliers: CGar; Chil; D&D; EWK; JWB; OGC; Rog; Suff; Tuck

Saxa
Suppliers: Bakk

Slenderette
Really outstanding for its heavy crop of thick fleshy stringless pods. Strong-growing variety which crops over a long period. (Sutt)
Suppliers: Rog

Sprite
Dark green, pencil shaped pods. Very suitable for freezing. (EWK)
Suppliers: CGar; EWK; Rog; SbS; Sutt

Sungold
Suppliers: Rog

Sunray
A highly appreciated variety for Market Growers as well as for Home Gardeners. Dark green pods which are excellent for deep freezing, stringless. (Brwn)
Suppliers: Brwn; Rog; Yate

Tavera
Suppliers: RSlu

Tendercrop
Long round pods, stringless, crisp and fleshy. They remain in good condition on the plants for a long time. (Unwi)
Suppliers: Unwi

Tendergreen
Fleshy, meaty pods which are stringless and fibreless with an excellent flavour. (T&M)
Suppliers: Barb; Brwn; Cart; CGar; D&D; EWK; Foth; John; JWB; Mole; OGC; Rog; SbS; SMM; Sutt; Toze; Tuck; VanH

The Prince
Long slim pods with a magnificent flavour. Excellent for freezing and one of the most widely grown varieties. (T&M)
Suppliers: Barb; Cart; CGar; Chil; D&D; Dob; EWK; Foth; JWB; Mars; Mole; OGC; Rog; SbS; Sutt; T&M; Unwi

Triomphe de Farcy
Suppliers: Bakk; Suff

Valja
Suppliers: Rog

Vilbel
Suppliers: T&M

Wachs Goldperle
A juicy, succulent bean, attractive in appearance and highly esteemed by Continental cooks. The productive plants carry clusters of golden-yellow,

round fleshy pods about 5in. long. These remain tender for a good length of time. Both seeds and flowers are white. (Dob)
 Suppliers: Dob
Synonyms
 Early Wax see Earlybird
 Flageolet Chevrier see Chevrier Vert
 Groene Flageolet see Chevrier Vert
 Mont d'Or Golden Butter see Mont d'Or
 St Andreas see Masterpiece

Garlic
Allium sativum
Very easy to grow, even in U.K. climates, and often becoming more prolific as it adapts to local conditions in successive seasons.
 Garlic
 Suppliers: Bakk; Dob; Foth; OGC; Poyn; Suff; Sutt; T&M
 Golden
 Suppliers: Futu
 Long Keeper
 Suppliers: Mars
 Pink
 Suppliers: Tuck
 Red Bulbed
 Suppliers: SMM
 Rocambole
 Suppliers: Poyn
 White Bulbed
 Suppliers: SMM
 White Pearl
 Suppliers: Rog

Good King Henry
Chenopodium bonus-henricus
A common enough perennial weed, but one with tasty and nutritious leaves. Also known as Mercury and Lincolnshire Spinach.
 Good King Henry
 Suppliers: CGar; Cham; Chil; D&D; EWK; Futu; OGC; Poyn; SMM; Suff; Unwi

Ground Cherry
Physalis pruinosa
Very like Cape Gooseberries, with fruits inside a papery husk.
Cossack's Pineapple
Suppliers: Futu

American Groundnut
Apios americana
American Groundnut
A hardy perennial vine that will climb several metres if given something to climb up. It produces strings of small ovoid tubers up to bantam egg size. The tubers are starchy and have a taste similar to potatoes and may be cooked by boiling, grilling or roasting. (Futu)
Suppliers: Futu

Horseradish Japanese
Wasabia japonica
Matsumi
Suppliers: Poyn

Huckleberry
Solanum burbankii
Mrs B's Garden Huckleberry
An annual which bears large quantities of sweet edible black berries ¾ cm. across, best used cooked in jams and pies &c. Although not of outstanding flavour, the plants are prolific, easy to grow, and their flavour mixes well with other fruits. They grow about 1m. tall, and once established require little attention, a good choice for low maintenance areas. (Futu)
Suppliers: Futu

Ice Plant
Mesembryanthemum spp
Although most people grow Mesembryanthemum for its flowers, the fleshy leaves make an interesting addition to summer salads.
Ice Plant
Suppliers: OGC; Suff

Jerusalem Artichoke
Helianthus tuberosus

An edible member of the Sunflower family, grown for its underground tubers. Makes an excellent cover crop.

Boston Red
Suppliers: Futu; SMM

Common
Suppliers: Mars

Cream
Suppliers: SMM

Dwarf Sunray
Suppliers: T&M

Fuseau
Suppliers: Futu; Mars

Jerusalem Artichoke
Suppliers: Bakk; Tuck

Silver Skinned
Suppliers: Futu

Jicama

Jicama
Suppliers: Chil

Kale
Brassica oleracea convar. *acephala*

F1 Arsis
Suppliers: RSlu

F1 Bornick
Suppliers: SbS

F1 Buffalo
Suppliers: Bree

F1 Darkibor
Suppliers: Brwn; Dob

Dwarf Green Curled
Suppliers: Bakk; Barb; Brwn; Butc; Cart; CGar; D&D; Dob; EWK; Foth; John; JWB; Mars; Mole; OGC; Rog; RSlu; SbS; Suff; T&M; Tuck; Unwi; Yate

F1 Fribor
Suppliers: Brwn; Butc; CGar; EWK; JWB; Mole; OGC; SbS; Toze; Tuck; Yate
Hungry Gap
Suppliers: Mars; Tuck
F1 Kobolt
Suppliers: Bree
Pentland Brig
Suppliers: CGar; EWK; JWB; Mars; OGC; SbS; SMM; Suff; Tuck; Unwi
Russian Red
Suppliers: Suff
F1 Showbor
Suppliers: Dob
Tall Green Curled
Suppliers: CGar; Mars; Mole; SbS; Sutt
Thousand Head
Suppliers: Barb; Dob; JWB; MAS; Suff; Sutt; Tuck; Unwi
Westland Autumn
Suppliers: Bakk; Dob
Westland Winter Toga
Suppliers: VanH
F1 Winterbor
Suppliers: Foth; SbS; Toze; Yate
Synonyms
Dwarf Green Curled Scotch see Dwarf Green Curled
Half Tall see Dwarf Green Curled
Tall Scotch Curled see Tall Green Curled
Westlandse Herfst see Westland Autumn

Kiwano
Kiwano
Suppliers: Chil

Kohlrabi
Brassica oleracea convar. *acephala*
Closely related to Kale, but grown for the edible swollen stems. The leaves can also be eaten.
Blaro
Suppliers: Bakk; Bree

Delicacy Purple
Suppliers: Bakk
F1 Dynamo
Suppliers: Yate
F1 Express Forcer
Suppliers: Bakk
F1 Kolpak
Suppliers: John; VanH
F1 Lanro
Suppliers: Bakk; Bree; Butc; Cart; Dob; Foth; Toze
Purple Vienna
Suppliers: Barb; Brwn; Butc; Chil; D&D; Dob; EWK; Foth; John; JWB; Mole; OGC; Rog; SbS; Suff; Sutt; Tuck
Roblau
Suppliers: Toze
Rolano
Suppliers: Dob
F1 Rowel
Suppliers: Mars; T&M; Unwi
Superschmelz
Suppliers: Bakk
White Vienna
Suppliers: Barb; Brwn; Butc; Chil; D&D; EWK; John; JWB; Mole; OGC; Rog; SbS; Sutt; Tuck
Synonyms
Delikatess Blauer see Delicacy Purple
Green Vienna see White Vienna

Komatsuna
Brassica rapa var. *pervidis* or var. *komatsuna*
Also known as Mustard Spinach and Spinach Mustard, which is confusing as it is neither a mustard nor a spinach, but a flowering rape, a kind of leafy turnip.
Green Boy
Suppliers: SMM
Komatsuna
Suppliers: Bakk; CGar; D&D; EWK; Futu; OGC; SbS; SMM; Suff
Senposai No 2
Suppliers: Dob

Tendergreen
Suppliers: Chil; T&M

Leaf Celery
Might this be a Stem Lettuce?
Krul
Suppliers: Foth
Leaf Celery
Suppliers: D&D; OGC

Leaf Tissue
Namenia spp
Namenia
Suppliers: Bakk

Leek
Allium porrum
There is no real distinction between pot leeks and blanching leeks, just that some varieties have a greater tendency to form a bulb at the base of the stem.
Alaska
An extremely winter hardy leek with dark blue-green foliage and stems 20-25cm. long. Shows strong regrowth in spring for harvest until May, and will not bolt readily during this period. (OGC)
Suppliers: Brwn; Butc; OGC; RSlu; SbS
Albinstar
Excellent variety for lifting late summer or early autumn. Long, slender shaft with light green foliage. Ideal for exhibition work. (EWK)
Suppliers: Bakk; CGar; D&D; EWK; JWB; OGC; Rog; SbS; Sutt; Tuck
Alita
Suppliers: RSlu
Alma
Suppliers: SbS
Argenta
An early Autumn Giant type that matures September-November from a sowing in April. Distinctive grey-green flag and thick shaft. Will often stand throughout the winter. (OGC)
Suppliers: Cart; Dob; OGC; RSlu; SbS; T&M

Armor
Suppliers: Yate
Autumn Giant Rami
Suppliers: Toze
Autumn Mammoth 2
Suppliers: Brwn; SbS; Toze
Autumn Mammoth 2 Walton Mammoth
Suppliers: Mars
Autumn Mammoth Greenstar
Suppliers: Toze
Autumn Triumphator
Suppliers: CGar
Bastion
Suppliers: Mole
Berdina
Suppliers: Bree
Blizzard
Suppliers: Mole; VanH
Blue Green Autumn
Suppliers: SbS
Blue Solaise
Suppliers: Bakk; SbS; Suff
Branta
Suppliers: Yate
Carentan
Robust, late autumn and winter leek which, provided it is not harvested too late, will yield a heavy crop. Strong stem, 20-30cm. long. (Bakk)
Suppliers: Bakk; OGC; Suff
Carina
Suppliers: Bree; Mars
Catalina
Very productive, giving large crops of long, heavy, non-bulbing leeks. (Foth)
Suppliers: Dob; SbS; Unwi
Coloma
Suppliers: SbS
Cortina
Combining exceptional winter hardiness and long standing ability with sturdy medium length stems, a pure white shaft and dark green leaves. Probably the best late. Maturing January to April. (T&M)
Suppliers: Bree; John; T&M

Derrick
Suppliers: EWK; SbS; VanH
Early Market
A very early maturing variety for use in autumn. (Sutt)
Suppliers: Sutt
Elephant
A true autumn leek, early-maturing. It has a short, thick stem which ensures an extremely high yield. Elephant will tolerate some frost without causing any problems. It is, however, advisable not to wait that long and to harvest before the frost sets in. (Bakk)
Suppliers: Bakk
Elina
Suppliers: SbS; Yate
Emperor
Suppliers: Toze
Giant Winter 3
Excellent late variety with good length stems. Slow to bolt. (EWK)
Suppliers: Bakk; Barb; Brwn; Butc; CGar; D&D; EWK; Mole; OGC; Rog; SbS; SMM; Yate
Giant Winter Granada
Suppliers: Toze
Glorina
Suppliers: Bree
Goldina
Suppliers: Yate
Goliath
A quality autumn maturing variety with a good blanch. (Brwn)
Suppliers: CGar; John; JWB; SbS; SMM; Toze; Tuck; Yate
Hannaball
Suppliers: SbS
Highland Giant
Hardy variety for lifting in January. Long shanks of pure white and will reach a good size when sown late March/early April. (VanH)
Suppliers: VanH
Jolant
Suppliers: Mole; Toze; VanH
Jubilee
Suppliers: SbS

Kajak
Long standing winter variety. Dark green foliage and very long white shaft. Has resistance to virus and leaf spot. (EWK)
Suppliers: Barb; CGar; D&D; EWK; Foth; OGC; Rog; SbS; Suff; Tuck
Kelvedon King
Suppliers: SbS
Kilima
Suppliers: RSlu; SbS
King Richard
Suppliers: Butc; Dob; Mars; SbS; Suff; Sutt; T&M; Unwi; Yate
Lavi
Suppliers: SbS
Libertas
A heavy cropping variety that is extremely hardy. White stem. Can be harvested until spring. (Bakk)
Suppliers: Bakk
Longbow
Suppliers: Toze
Longina
Suppliers: Bree
Lyon
Good all round variety for autumn use. (EWK)
Suppliers: Barb; D&D; EWK; Foth; John; JWB; MAS; OGC; Rog; SbS; SMM; Sutt; T&M; VanH
Malabar
Suppliers: SbS
Mammoth Blanch
A superior exhibition variety with extra long blanch. Specimens grown by amateurs have attained over 5lbs weight and 100 cubic ins. Exceptionally thick with broad flag. (Rob)
Suppliers: CGar; JWB; Rob
Mammoth Pot
A true Pot leek, very thick, with short blanch of approximately 5 ins. (13cm.) Bred for the exhibitor but yet retaining good flavour with tight flesh. One of the easiest leeks to grow, very frost hardy. (Rob)
Suppliers: CGar; Rob

Musselburgh
Harvest December-April. A most reliable and versatile variety which has been justifiably popular for many years. (OGC)
   Suppliers: Barb; Brwn; Cart; CGar; Chil; D&D; Dob; EWK; Foth; John; JWB; Mars; MAS; Mole; OGC; Rog; SbS; SMM; Sutt; T&M; Tuck; Unwi; VanH
Odin
   Suppliers: SbS
Pancho
Early maturing, yet will stand into mid-winter. Long, crisp, white blanched stems of excellent flavour. Ideal for slicing in late salads, or for conventional cooking. (Dob)
   Suppliers: Dob; Toze
Pot
A real exhibition strain. With careful attention will grow to an immense size. (EWK)
   Suppliers: Butc; EWK; JWB; Rog; SMM; VanH
Prelina
   Suppliers: Bree
Prenora
   Suppliers: Yate
Profina
   Suppliers: Bree
Selecta
   Suppliers: SbS
Siegfried Frost
   Suppliers: Yate
Snowstar
   Suppliers: Dob; Foth; John; SbS; Toze
Snowstar B
   Suppliers: Mole
Splendid
An excellent autumn and early winter leek that does not bulb at the base. It produces uniform blanched shafts about 12cm. (5in.) long, 2.5cm. (1in.) diameter. (Unwi)
   Suppliers: SbS; Suff; Toze; Unwi
Startrack
A fairly long, slender variety, recommended for early autumn cultivation. Of all Autumn Giant selections Startrack has the darkest leaves. (Bakk)
   Suppliers: Bakk; Brwn; John; Toze; Yate

Sterna
Suppliers: Brwn
Thor
Early type with very long shafts and medium green foliage. (EWK)
Suppliers: SbS
Tilina
Suppliers: Bree; Toze
Titan
An early summer leek, forming long stems. However, Titan does not tolerate frost. This variety has a very agreeable, aromatic flavour. (Bakk)
Suppliers: Bakk; SbS
Toledo
Suppliers: Toze
Tropita
Late summer and early autumn variety. Extremely long shanks. (EWK)
Suppliers: EWK; SbS
Varna
Suppliers: RSlu
Verina
Suppliers: Bree; SbS; Unwi
Wila
An extremely hardy leek with dark blue-green leaves. Stems straight and thick, increasing in weight in late winter and remaining in condition until May. (Mars)
Suppliers: Mars
Winora
Suppliers: Yate
Winter
A fine growing trench leek, very dark green leaves, frost hardy. (Rob)
Suppliers: Rob
Winter Crop
Outstanding late-maturing, extra-hardy variety with large white stems and very dark foliage. Stands well for use until April. (Sutt)
Suppliers: Sutt
Wintra
Suppliers: EWK
Yates Empire
A very good leek with thick stems. Matures late, standing well into April. (Unwi)
Suppliers: SbS; Unwi

Synonyms
    Autumn Giant see Goliath
    Autumn Mammoth see Goliath
    Bleu de Solaise see Blue Solaise
    Bluestar see Giant Winter 3
    Cobham Empire see Yates Empire
    Gennevilliers Splendid see Splendid
    Herfstreuzen see Goliath
    Hiverbleu see Libertas
    Longstanton see Odin
    Malabare see Malabar
    Monstuoso di Carentan see Carentan
    Prizetaker see Lyon
    St Victor see Blue Solaise
    The Lyon see Lyon
    Walton Mammoth see Autumn Mammoth 2
    Winterreuzen see Giant Winter 3

Lettuce
Lactuca sativa
Generally divided into three main categories, Cos, Head and Leaf.
    Ambassador
        Suppliers: SbS
    Bambi
        Suppliers: Foth
    Bastion
    A new crisp head variety for greenhouse production during the winter months. Forms large firm hearts which are welcome as an additional fresh vegetable for Christmas salads. (John)
        Suppliers: John; Toze
    Besson
        Suppliers: Bakk
    Capitan
        Suppliers: Toze
    Clarisse
        Suppliers: Toze
    Cosmic
        Suppliers: Toze

Dark Green Boston
Suppliers: SbS
Diana
Suppliers: Toze
Dynasty
Suppliers: D&D; EWK; OGC
Favourite
Suppliers: Bakk; SbS
Feltham King
Suppliers: SbS
Hudson
Suppliers: Mole
Joanita
Suppliers: Toze
Karlo
Suppliers: Toze
Kelly's
A crisp variety with bright green leaves. Sow Oct/Nov for harvest in Mar/Apr. (OGC)
Suppliers: Barb; Brwn; EWK; Mars; Mole; OGC; Rog; Tuck; Unwi
Kim
Suppliers: Toze
Kirsten
Suppliers: Toze
Mayfair
Suppliers: Toze
Novita
Suppliers: Brwn; EWK
Pascal
For autumn, winter and spring cutting. Quick growing, thick leaves. Performed among the best in many international trials. Resistant to Bremia races 1, 2, 3, 4, 5 and 6. (Brwn)
Suppliers: Mole; Tuck
Pavane
A little Gem or 'Sucrine' type. Pavane forms a small cos-like head with a dense heart. Slightly darker than Little Gem, Pavane is a very uniform variety with added LMV resistance. (Bree)
Suppliers: Bree
Perlane
Suppliers: SbS

Prestine
    Suppliers: SbS
Ravel
Emerald green heads for glasshouse use from October to early May. (EWK)
    Suppliers: EWK; Mole
Renania
Forms a robust, tender head which is very slow to run to seed. A true summer lettuce, deservedly called 'the pride of every good gardener'. (Bakk)
    Suppliers: Bakk
Rosana
    Suppliers: Toze
Rossalita
    Suppliers: Bree; T&M
Sangria
    Suppliers: Sutt
Targa
Spring cutting variety with large heads of medium green. Excellent head protection during growing period. High Bremia resistance. Sow late Autumn or very early Spring. (EWK)
    Suppliers: EWK
Zodiac
    Suppliers: Cart; Mole
Synonyms
    Batavia Blonde see Favourite
    Blonde de Paris see Favourite
    Gloire de Nantes see Feltham King

Lettuce Cos
Angela
Just as sweet and tender as Little Gem but much easier to separate leaves for garnish, salads etc. Mildew resistant. Virus tolerant. (T&M)
    Suppliers: Bree; T&M
Apache
Cream, pink and green hearts. Crisp and sweet with bronzy red outer leaf. Pick slightly immature for the best colour. (T&M)
    Suppliers: T&M
Balloon
A heavy weight cos, light green with a brown tinge to the leaves. (OGC)
    Suppliers: CGar; EWK; JWB; OGC; SbS
Bubbles
    Suppliers: Dob; Toze

Carten
Suppliers: SbS
Corsair
Flat dark green leaves with strong flavour. (SMM)
Suppliers: Dob; Toze
Corsaro
Suppliers: RSlu
Dark Green Cos
Darker green and slower growing than Lobjoits, it is outstanding in later summer crops and is very resistant to tipburn and bolting. LMV tolerant. (Bree)
Suppliers: Bree; JWB; SbS
Jewel
Solid dark heart like a larger Little Gem. Very sweet flavour. Sow spring or autumn. (Mars)
Suppliers: Sutt; Toze
Little Gem
A cross between cos and cabbage lettuce with some of the benefits of both. Can be sown in the open throughout the growing season and lends itself well to being sown in the early autumn and cloched during the winter. (OGC)
Suppliers: Barb; Bree; Brwn; Cart; CGar; D&D; Dob; EWK; Foth; John; JWB; Mars; Mole; OGC; Rog; RSlu; SbS; SMM; Suff; Sutt; T&M; Toze; Tuck; Unwi; VanH; Yate
Lobjoits Green Cos
Tall, deep green hearts, very crisp. Self-folding. (Mars)
Suppliers: Barb; Bree; D&D; EWK; John; JWB; Mars; Mole; OGC; Rog; SbS; Sutt; Toze; Tuck; VanH; Yate
Paris Island
Suppliers: SbS
Paris White
Much improved cos type with medium large compact heads. Will stand for a long time when ready to cut. (EWK)
Suppliers: Barb; Cart; Chil; D&D; EWK; JWB; Rog; SbS
Romance
Makes a substantial, tightly folded head with crisp, sweet heart. (Dob)
Suppliers: Bree; Dob
Rouge d'Hiver
A good tasty cos with long red pointed leaves. Very hardy. Sow late summer-autumn or early spring. An old French variety and very rare. (Suff)
Suppliers: Suff

Toledo
Suppliers: RSlu; T&M
Valdor
Overwinter greenhouse type. This can also be sown outside. Attractive light green heads with good resistance to bolting. Sow in Aug/Sep. (OGC)
Suppliers: Barb; Cart; CGar; Dob; EWK; JWB; Mole; OGC; Rog; SbS; SMM; Sutt; Tuck
Valmaine
A cos type used for cut and come again, giving two crops from one sowing. Very productive and the individual leaves are deliciously crisp. Resistant to some races of mildew and particularly useful for summer/autumn use. (OGC)
Suppliers: EWK; JWB; Mole; OGC; SbS; Toze; Yate
Wallop
This semi-cos type yields extra large and densely packed heads. The leaves stand quite upright and are crisp and tender with a sweet flavour. (Foth)
Suppliers: Foth
Winter Density
Larger than Little Gem; a very good crisp variety, much used for autumn sowing. (OGC)
Suppliers: Barb; Brwn; CGar; Chil; D&D; Dob; EWK; Foth; John; JWB; Mars; Mole; OGC; Rog; SbS; Sutt; Toze; Unwi; VanH
Synonyms
Ballon see Balloon
Blonde Maraichere see Paris White
Craquerelle du Midi see Winter Density
Grise Maraichere see Lobjoits Green Cos
lobj see Lobjoits Green Cos
Sucrine see Little Gem
Val d'Orge see Valdor

Lettuce Head
All The Year Round
A butterhead type for successional sowings from spring to autumn. (OGC)
Suppliers: Barb; Cart; CGar; Chil; Dob; EWK; Foth; John; JWB; Mars; OGC; Rog; SbS; SMM; Sutt; T&M; Tuck; Unwi
Arctic King
Suppliers: Barb; CGar; D&D; Dob; EWK; JWB; MAS; Rog; SbS; Sutt; Tuck; VanH
Avoncrisp
Suppliers: Barb; CGar; EWK; JWB; Mars; Mole; OGC; Rog; SbS; Tuck; Yate

Avondefiance
Dark green in colour. Useful for summer sowing due to its high resistance to mildew. Popular with commercial growers, and successful in warm climates. (OGC)
    Suppliers: Brwn; CGar; Dob; EWK; JWB; Mars; Mole; OGC; Rog; SbS; Sutt; Tuck; VanH; Yate
Baltic
    Suppliers: Mars; RSlu
Beatrice
A new generation of lettuce. Early, easy to grow with excellent mildew and root aphid resistance, superb vigour and fast crop growth. Ideal as an early Iceberg, with bright green solid crunchy heads and short internal stalk. (T&M)
    Suppliers: Mole; T&M
Bellona
    Suppliers: Yate
Berlo
    Suppliers: Toze
Borough Wonder
Excellent Summer variety for a regular sowing. Large, pale green, tender heads. (EWK)
    Suppliers: Barb; CGar; EWK; Rog
Bruna di Germania
Small red/brown hardy lettuce for overwintering, growing to 8in. Does better with some protection, i.e. a cold frame, or tunnel. (Suff)
    Suppliers: Suff
Buttercrunch
Dark green with compact heads which stands well. The central leaves are very crisp and it is resistant to hot weather. One of the best garden lettuces. (OGC)
    Suppliers: CGar; D&D; Dob; EWK; Foth; John; JWB; OGC; Rog; SbS; Suff; T&M; Unwi; VanH
Capitol
The best Iceberg for spring cropping in the cold greenhouse. Firm, heavy, crisp and crunchy heads. (T&M)
    Suppliers: T&M; Toze
Carlane
    Suppliers: Yate
Chaperon
    Suppliers: Brwn

Cindy
Suppliers: Mole
Clarion
Thick leaved variety cropping throughout the Summer. Bremia resistant.
(EWK)
Suppliers: Brwn; EWK; Mole; SbS; Toze
Cobham Green
Similar to New Market, but dark green colour. (JWB)
Suppliers: JWB; Mole; SbS; Toze
Columbus
Greenhouse type. Fast growing. Bright green thick textured leaves. Sow late
August to mid-February for late October-early May cropping. (Dob)
Suppliers: Cart; CGar; Dob; EWK
Continuity
Only suitable for sowing in the spring and summer, it is very long standing.
Distinct reddish brown in colour, it improves the appearance of a mixed
salad. It is claimed that the colour deters pigeons. (OGC)
Suppliers: Barb; CGar; D&D; Dob; EWK; JWB; OGC; Rog; SbS; Tuck;
Unwi
Crestana
Suppliers: Bree; T&M
Crispino
Suppliers: RSlu
Cynthia
A crisp, tasty butterhead type that is a little later to harvest than Kwiek.
(Foth)
Suppliers: Unwi
Dandie
Autumn sowing, glasshouse variety for cutting March and April. Well filled
heads of good colour. (EWK)
Suppliers: CGar; EWK
Daphne
Suppliers: Mole; Toze; Yate
Debby
Extremely versatile. It can be sown indoors from January, outdoors from
March to late July, to crop from May until early November. It is noted for
producing full, firm heads in mid-summer, when many other varieties bolt
easily. Resistance to lettuce root aphid, mildew and lettuce mosaic virus.
(Mars)
Suppliers: Mars; Unwi

Dolly
A large, dark green, butterhead variety suitable for growing in a cold or slightly heated greenhouse. Sow from October-January for February-April harvesting. Resistant to mildew and tipburn. (Sutt)
Suppliers: Unwi
E6400
Suppliers: Yate
El Toro
Hard, dense, crisp, crunchy head. Very quick growing, yet mature heads stand till October. (T&M)
Suppliers: T&M
Elvira
Suppliers: John
Fivia
Suppliers: T&M
Grande
Suppliers: RSlu
Great Lakes 659
The well-known American crisphead lettuce which forms a real 'cabbage' that is not prone to bolt. Can be kept in the refrigerator for quite some time. (Bakk)
Suppliers: Bakk; Brwn; CGar; EWK; JWB; Mars; MAS; Mole; OGC; SbS; SMM; Unwi
Great Lakes Mesa 659
Suppliers: SbS
Grosse Blonde Paresseuse
A slow-bolting summer lettuce producing large, light green heads. (Bakk)
Suppliers: Bakk
Hilde II
Is at present considered one of the most cultivated varieties. Produces solid, healthy heads, tender and with a very fine flavour. Recommended! (Bakk)
Suppliers: Bakk; Cart; Mars; SbS; Sutt; Unwi; VanH
Iceberg
This is essentially a summer lettuce with pale green leaves, slightly red tinged with large crisp white hearts. (OGC)
Suppliers: Barb; CGar; EWK; John; JWB; Mole; OGC; Rog; SbS; SMM; T&M; Tuck; VanH

Impala
Impala is a short day lettuce, producing high quality heads with a well closed base. Suggested sowing period September to November. Optimum harvest period December-April. Bremia resistance. (RSlu)
   Suppliers: Yate
Imperial Winter
A hardy outdoor variety for autumn sowing and cutting in the spring. (OGC)
   Suppliers: Bakk; Barb; CGar; EWK; John; OGC; Rog; SbS
Ithaca
A crisp variety, slow bolting, resistant against mildew and tipburn. (Mole)
   Suppliers: Mole; SbS; Toze
Jarino
   Suppliers: Bakk
Kares
A really excellent variety for mid-summer to early autumn use. Excellent dark green lettuce, resistant to almost all diseases, and slow to bolt. Sow from March onwards. (VanH)
   Suppliers: VanH
Kelvin
   Suppliers: Mole; RSlu
King Crown
Superb thick, dark green leaves and large solid heads. Suitable for Spring, late Summer and Autumn sowing and does well in all soils. (EWK)
   Suppliers: EWK; SbS
Kloek
A butterhead type for overwintering. Sow Oct/Nov for harvest in Mar/Apr. (OGC)
   Suppliers: Barb; CGar; D&D; EWK; OGC; Rog; SbS
Kwiek
A butterhead variety for cutting in Nov/Dec. Sow in late August. (OGC)
   Suppliers: Barb; CGar; D&D; EWK; Foth; JWB; OGC; Rog; SbS; Sutt; VanH
Kylie
   Suppliers: Bree
Lake Nyah
A very uniform bright green crisp lettuce of good quality, especially recommended for July and August cutting when well developed medium-sized hearts will be produced. Stands well and is a fine variety of the Iceberg type. (Sutt)
   Suppliers: CGar; SbS

Lakeland
The best iceberg lettuce for spring, summer or autumn. It comes into cut earlier than most and is ideal for spring cropping in frames as well as outdoor. It is resistant to mildew and lettuce root aphid. (Mars)
    Suppliers: Brwn; Cart; Dob; Foth; Mars; Toze; Unwi

Lilian
Firm, well-wrapped heads of bright green with generous hearts of crisp-sweet taste. Ideal for successional sowings either in the open or under cloches. (Dob)
    Suppliers: Dob; Toze

Magnet
Glasshouse type for cold production in late Autumn. (EWK)
    Suppliers: John

Malika
Outdoor crisp lettuce valued for its earliness, unlike some other early varieties, 'coning' in Malika is virtually unknown. Performs very well from early production under Pholene as well as from unprotected crops. LMV tolerant. (Bree)
    Suppliers: Bree; SbS; Unwi

Marmer
Very firm, crisp, heavy heads. Sow Aug/Sep, harvest January. Sow Nov/Jan, harvest April on. Grows best in cool conditions. (T&M)
    Suppliers: Suff

Marshall
Large iceberg type lettuces with full heads and slightly bubbled, succulent leaves. (Foth)
    Suppliers: Yate

Massa
    Suppliers: SbS

May King
An autumn planting lettuce, it can be equally successful when planted in the spring or summer. Mid-green, slightly tinged with red, early and hardy, it is first class for frame, cold greenhouse or outdoor growing. (OGC)
    Suppliers: Bakk; Barb; Dob; EWK; JWB; SbS; Sutt

Merveille des Quatre Saisons
Red leaved lettuce with curled leaves. Can be sown all the year round, but best results from spring and autumn sowing. Solid heart and very good flavour. (Suff)
    Suppliers: Bree; Mole; OGC; SMM; Suff; Toze

Michelle
    Suppliers: Yate

Minetto
Suppliers: SbS
Mirian
Suppliers: Bree
Musette
An excellent mid-green variety for summer and autumn, Musette is uniform with a large head. It shows resistance to downy mildew and mosaic virus. (OGC)
Suppliers: Mole; OGC; SbS; Sutt
Nancy
Suppliers: Mole
Neckarriesen
Produces tender, large, bright green heads. A top quality lettuce with an excellent flavour, suitable for spring and summer cultivation. The seed is virus-free, so it will give an extremely high yield. (Bakk)
Suppliers: Bakk
Novita
Curly lettuce with a very well-filled head. Crispy texture and special flavour. Easier to grow than other varieties because of its resistance to tipburn. For sowing from September to mid-February. (Mars)
Suppliers: Dob; Mars; Rog; VanH
Oresto
Suppliers: RSlu
Pandorian
Suppliers: Bree
Pantra
Suppliers: Bree
Parella
One of the hardiest winter lettuces grown in the mountainous region of Northern Italy. Survived -15°C in a cold winter. Broadcast autumn or spring and thin to 4-6 in. apart. Very tiny neat lettuce forming small heart or rosette. Cut and come again or harvest whole plant. (Suff)
Suppliers: Suff
Parella Red
A decorative red version of the compact and hardy Parella Green. When left to bolt it makes a most decorative plant good enough for the flower garden. (Suff)
Suppliers: Suff
Pennlake
Suppliers: Brwn; Mole; SbS; Toze; Yate

Rachel
Suppliers: Brwn
Red Fire
Suppliers: CGar; EWK; SMM
Red Valeria
The most intense red with a uniform mound of fine serrated loose leaves.
The centre can become slightly green/blonde. Looks so attractive and tastes
quite exceptional. (Foth)
Suppliers: Foth
Regina dei Ghiacci
Crisphead lettuce for summer use; slow to run to seed. Sow March to July,
thinning to 8-10in. apart. Attractive foliage. (Suff)
Suppliers: Suff
Reskia
The variety for all season cropping from Spring to Autumn. Butterhead type
with firm, large mid-green heads. (EWK)
Suppliers: EWK; JWB; Mole; Rog; Tuck; VanH
Ritmo
Suppliers: Yate
Rosanna
Suppliers: Mole
Rossa Fruilana
Forms an attractive frilly leaved red tinged heart. Most decorative in summer
salads. Like many lettuce varieties it will resprout from its base if cut young.
(Suff)
Suppliers: Suff
Rossimo
Suppliers: Foth
Rouge Grenobloise
Crisp, heavy lettuce with a very pleasant flavour. Hardly or not at all bolting
and, therefore, very suitable for sowing in summer. (Bakk)
Suppliers: Bakk
Rougette du Midi
A most attractive small reddish leaved lettuce. Sow in Autumn for winter
and spring lettuce. Very crisp and tasty. (Suff)
Suppliers: Suff
Ruth
Suppliers: Brwn
S 0254
Suppliers: Bree

S 0256

Suppliers: Bree

S1179

Suppliers: Bree

Sabrina

Suppliers: Foth; Mole; Toze; Yate

Saladin

An excellent crisphead variety, producing solid iceberg type heads, light green in colour. Slow to bolt in hot weather and useful throughout the spring and summer. (OGC)

Suppliers: Bakk; Bree; Brwn; CGar; D&D; Dob; EWK; Foth; John; JWB; Mole; OGC; Rog; RSlu; SbS; Toze; Tuck; Unwi; VanH; Yate

Salina

Mid green butterhead variety for summer production or protected cropping under polythene/glass. (CGar)

Suppliers: Mole

Santis

Suppliers: John

Sheena

Suppliers: Bree

Sigmaball

Large, round, mid-green hearts of slightly crisp texture and fine flavour. Stands in condition over a long period, and is resistant to tipburn and root aphid. Sow outdoors April-June in succession. (Sutt)

Suppliers: Sutt

Sigmahead

Of crisp texture and erect growth. Can be grown closely and still produce good hearts. Resistant to tipburn, botrytis and root aphid. (Sutt)

Suppliers: Sutt

Sitonia

For harvesting late spring, summer and autumn. Excellent resistance to tipburn and bolting. Resistant to Bremia. (Brwn)

Suppliers: Mole

Standwell

Suppliers: Bakk

Suzan

Soft butterhead type with good compact heads. Quick maturity for early Summer use. (EWK)

Suppliers: CGar; EWK; JWB; Mole; Rog; SbS; Sutt; Tuck

Target

Suppliers: Sutt; Yate

Telda
Suppliers: RSlu
Timo
Suppliers: Yate
Tires
A very attractive dark green lettuce with medium large firm heads. Develops quickly and can be grown throughout the season for cutting in summer and autumn. Excellent in frames and cloches for earlier crops. (Sutt)
Suppliers: Sutt
Titania
Suppliers: Toze; Yate
Tom Thumb
An early dwarf variety which deserves greater popularity. It hearts quickly and is compact and long standing, thus cutting down on wastage. (OGC)
Suppliers: Barb; Brwn; Cart; CGar; Chil; Dob; EWK; Foth; John; JWB; Mars; Mole; OGC; Rog; SbS; Suff; Sutt; T&M; Tuck; Unwi
Unrivalled
Medium-sized hearts. Sow outdoors in spring and summer. Also excellent for January-February sowing under glass for transplanting outdoors. (Sutt)
Suppliers: Chil; EWK; John; JWB; Mole; OGC; Rog; SbS; Sutt
Vicky
Suppliers: Mole; Toze; Yate
Virginia
Suppliers: Toze
Warpath
Bred in England. A cross between a cos and an Iceberg with eating qualities from both and the crunchy leaves form a small heart. Faster to mature than an Iceberg it can be sown at up to twice the density. It has good bolt resistance. (Foth)
Suppliers: Brwn; Foth; Sutt
Webbs Wonderful
One of the most popular of all lettuces, crisp, solid, large, long standing and of excellent quality. (OGC)
Suppliers: Barb; Cart; CGar; Chil; D&D; Dob; EWK; Foth; John; JWB; Mars; Mole; OGC; Rog; SbS; SMM; Sutt; T&M; Tuck; Unwi; VanH
Windermere
An outstanding quality crisphead. Medium sized heads, very uniform growth. (OGC)
Suppliers: CGar; D&D; EWK; JWB; OGC; Rog; SbS; Sutt
Synonyms
Attraction see Unrivalled

Blonde a Bord Rouge see Iceberg
British Hilde see Hilde II
Constant Heart see Hilde II
De Verrieres see Imperial Winter
Fortune see Hilde II
Great Lakes see Great Lakes 659
Kagraner Sommer see Standwell
Maikonig see May King
May Queen see May King
Meraviglia delle Quattro Stagioni see Merveille des Quatre Saisons
Merveille d'Hiver see Imperial Winter
New Market see Unrivalled
New York see Webbs Wonderful
Plena see Hilde II
Poulton Market see Hilde II
Supermarket see Hilde II
Trocadero Improved see Unrivalled
Winter Crop see Imperial Winter
Winter Marvel see Imperial Winter

Lettuce Leaf

Americana Bruna
Suppliers: Bakk
Bataser
Suppliers: Bree
Biscia Rossa
A very pretty lettuce with red tinged leaves from Italy. May be used for cut and come again or allowed to grow on. (Suff)
Suppliers: Suff
Carnival
A loose leaf lettuce which forms large heads but does not heart. Glossy green leaves with a rosy tinge. Super crisp leaf. (OGC)
Suppliers: OGC; Sutt
Everest
Suppliers: John
Grand Rapids
Suppliers: SbS
Little Leprechaun
Suppliers: EWK
Lolla Bionda
Suppliers: Bree; Dob; Foth; Mars; Mole; Toze; Yate

Lollo Biando Casablanca
Suppliers: RSlu
Lollo Green
Suppliers: Suff
Lollo Mixed
A delightful and attractive mixture of the popular Italian Lollo type lettuce, including the bright green Lollo Verde, with Rossa for extra colour in salads and garnishes. (Unwi)
Suppliers: Unwi
Lollo Rosso
The attractively fringed and crinkled pale green leaves with a crimson edge form a loose heart. Crispness and flavour far better than all other looseleaf lettuces. Three or four sowings will last the whole summer. (Mars)
Suppliers: Bakk; Bree; Cart; CGar; Chil; Dob; EWK; Foth; JWB; Mars; Mole; OGC; SbS; Suff; Sutt; T&M; Toze; Tuck; Unwi
Lollo Rosso Astina
Suppliers: John; RSlu
Lollo Rosso Lovina
A superior selection of this popular type of lettuce. It forms a solid, ball shaped plant with attractive red-brown, deeply lobed and frilled leaves each with a contrasting pale green centre. It enhances both the appearance and flavour of a salad.(John)
Suppliers: Yate
Pablo
Suppliers: Foth; John; RSlu; T&M
Raisa
Suppliers: John
Red Sails
Distinct All-American Selection winner. Highly recommended and nutritional, it is a loose leaf type and, with a greater leaf area exposed to the sun, has six times the vitamin A than of other crisp head varieties. The bronzy-red leaves greatly enhance a salad. (John)
Suppliers: John
Riccia a folglia di Quercia
Suppliers: Suff
Rusty
Suppliers: Toze

Salad Bowl

A very useful lettuce quite different from other varieties, as it has no heart, and a few leaves can be taken without uprooting the whole plant. (OGC)

Suppliers: Barb; Butc; Cart; CGar; D&D; Dob; EWK; John; JWB; Mars; OGC; Rog; SbS; Suff; Sutt; Tuck; VanH

Salad Bowl Greenwich

Suppliers: Bree

Salad Bowl Mixed

Both the colours of oak-leaf lettuce together, with this crisp and tender non-hearting variety. Leaves can be picked a few at a time. Hardly ever bolts. (Foth)

Suppliers: Foth; Unwi

Salad Bowl Red

A pretty form of Salad Bowl Green. Ideal for small gardens, will last throughout the summer if picked regularly. (Suff)

Suppliers: Bakk; Barb; Brwn; Butc; CGar; D&D; Dob; EWK; JWB; Mole; OGC; Rog; SbS; Suff; Sutt; Toze; Tuck; VanH

Salad Bowl Red Kamino

Similar plant type to Salad Bowl, with indented oak leaf but with strong red coloration. Suitable for outdoor cropping in Spring, Summer and Autumn. (Bree)

Suppliers: Bree

Salad Bowl Red Rebosa

Suppliers: RSlu

Salad Bowl Red Selma

Suppliers: Yate

Sigla

Suppliers: Brwn

Soprane

Suppliers: Yate

Valeria

This versatile variety, is a counterpart of Lollo Rossa and Lollo Bionda, producing intensive red leaf colour when grown during the winter months in a frost-free greenhouse or frame. Also superb when grown outdoors during Spring and Summer. (Dob)

Suppliers: Dob

Synonyms
    Lollo Red see Lollo Rosso

Lettuce Stem
Lactuca sativa var. *augustana*
Celtuce is one name given to this variety of lettuce, grown for the swollen stem.

Celtuce
Halfway between celery and lettuce, the stems and leaves are excellent alternatives and very tasty. (Foth). Celtuce is not a cross, but a type of lettuce grown primarily for its swollen stem.
    Suppliers: Butc; CGar; Cham; Chil; EWK; JWB; OGC; SbS; SMM; Sutt; T&M; VanH

Woh Sun
    Suppliers: Suff

Lettuce Thai
Thai Lettuce
    Suppliers: Suff

Mangel
Beta vulgaris
Brooks Red Intermediate
    Suppliers: JWB
Prizewinner
    Suppliers: EWK; OGC; Rog

Marrow
Cucurbita pepo
There is much confusion over marrows, squashes, and courgettes, or zucchini. All these marrows can be picked small as courgettes.

F1 Acceste
    Suppliers: RSlu; T&M
All Green Bush
    Suppliers: Barb; Butc; Chil; D&D; EWK; Foth; John; JWB; Mole; OGC; Rog; SbS; SMM; Unwi; VanH
F1 Altea
    Suppliers: Bree

F1 Ambassador
Suppliers: CGar; Dob; EWK; Foth; John; Mars; Mole; OGC; RSlu; SbS; Toze; Tuck; Yate

F1 Arlesa
Suppliers: Bree

Bianco Friulano
Suppliers: Suff

Brimmer
Suppliers: CGar; SbS; T&M

Burpee Golden Zucchini
Suppliers: Butc; CGar; D&D; EWK; OGC; Rog; SbS; Sutt

Bush Green
Suppliers: JWB

Bush White
Suppliers: JWB

Clarella
Suppliers: OGC; Suff

F1 Clarita
Suppliers: Unwi

Cobham Green Bush
Suppliers: Bree; Toze

F1 Crusader
Suppliers: Brwn; Toze

Custard White
Suppliers: Butc; CGar; Dob; EWK; JWB; Mole; OGC; Rog; SbS; SMM; Suff; Tuck

Custard Yellow
Suppliers: SbS

F1 Defender
Suppliers: Toze

F1 Diamond
Suppliers: Bakk; Mole; SbS

F1 Elite
Suppliers: Toze

F1 Gold Rush
Suppliers: Bakk; Bree; Chil; Dob; Foth; John; JWB; Mars; Mole; RSlu; SbS; Suff; T&M; Toze; Unwi; Yate

Green Bush Improved
Suppliers: Sutt

Green Gem
Suppliers: SbS
F1 Greyzini
Suppliers: Butc; EWK; Mole; Rog; RSlu; SbS; Toze; Tuck; Yate
F1 Jackpot
Suppliers: SbS
Kingsize
Suppliers: T&M
Long Green Bush
Suppliers: Barb; Brwn; CGar; Chil; D&D; EWK; Foth; John; OGC; Rog; RSlu; SbS; SbS; T&M; Tuck; Unwi; VanH; Yate
Long Green Bush 2
Suppliers: Cart; Dob; Mars
Long Green Bush 3 Smallpak
Suppliers: Sutt
Long Green Trailing
Suppliers: Barb; Butc; CGar; D&D; Dob; EWK; Foth; John; JWB; Mars; Mole; OGC; Rog; SbS; Sutt; T&M; Tuck; Unwi; VanH
Long White Bush
Suppliers: Bakk
Long White Trailing
Suppliers: Dob; JWB; SbS
F1 Market King
Suppliers: SbS
Minipak
Suppliers: Butc; CGar; EWK; Rog; SbS; Suff; VanH
F1 Moreno
Suppliers: Foth; Mars; Yate
F1 Onyx
Suppliers: SbS
Prepak
Suppliers: SbS
F1 President
Suppliers: Mole; SbS; Yate
F1 Raven
Suppliers: Bree; Foth
Rondo de Nice
Suppliers: OGC; Suff; T&M
F1 Saracen
Suppliers: Brwn; Toze

F1 Storr's Green
Suppliers: Barb; Bree; Butc; Cart; CGar; D&D; Dob; EWK; John; JWB; Mars; Mole; OGC; Rog; SbS; SMM; Suff; Sutt; Toze; Unwi; VanH; Yate

F1 Supremo
Suppliers: Bree; Dob; T&M

Table Dainty
Suppliers: Butc; Chil; JWB; SbS; Sutt

F1 Tarmino
Suppliers: Unwi

Tender and True
Suppliers: JWB; Sutt

F1 Tiger Cross
Suppliers: Cart; Foth; Sutt; T&M; Toze

Vegetable Spaghetti
Suppliers: Butc; CGar; D&D; Dob; EWK; JWB; OGC; SbS; SMM; Sutt; T&M; Tuck; Unwi

White Bush
Suppliers: Barb; CGar; Dob; Rog; SbS

F1 Zebra Cross
Suppliers: Mars; Mole; Toze; Yate

Zucchini
Suppliers: EWK; Rog; Sutt; Toze

F1 Zucchini Blondy
Suppliers: T&M

F1 Zucchini Elite
Suppliers: SbS

F1 Zucchini Spineless Beauty
Suppliers: T&M

F1 Zucchini True French
Suppliers: T&M

Synonyms
Early Gem see Storr's Green
Emerald Cross see Greyzini
Golden Zucchini see Burpee Golden
Green Bush see Long Green Bush
Green Bush F1 Hybrid see Storr's Green
Green Trailing see Long Green Trailing
Long Green Striped see Long Green Trailing
Marco see Ambassador
Superlative see Blenheim Orange
Tondo do Nizza see Rondo de Nice

Zucchini F1 see Storr's Green

Mashua
Tropaeolum tuberosum
Another Lost Vegetable of the Incas, with gorgeous flowers and edible tubers.

Mashua
A close relative of the garden nasturtium which is cultivated in the high Andes for its edible tubers, this climbing perennial will reach over 2m. if given support, otherwise it forms a prostrate mass of weed-supressing foliage. The tubers are about the size of small potatoes and are conical in shape, having a yellow skin with numerous purple flecks. Eaten raw, they have a hot peppery flavour, with a faint vanilla-like aroma. When cooked, the peppery taste disappears and the vanilla taste becomes sweeter and stronger — definitely an acquired taste. (Futu)
Suppliers: Futu; Poyn

Melon
Cucumis melo
F1 Amber Nectar
Suppliers: T&M
F1 Ananas
Suppliers: Bakk; CGar; EWK
F1 Aroma
Suppliers: CGar; EWK
Blenheim Orange
Suppliers: Barb; CGar; D&D; EWK; JWB; OGC; Rog; SMM; Sutt; Unwi
Charentais
Suppliers: Brwn; Butc; CGar; Foth; Sutt; Toze; VanH
Dutch Net
Suppliers: CGar
Early Dawn
Suppliers: Toze
F1 Early Sweet
Suppliers: Sutt
Emerald Gem
Suppliers: Sutt
F1 Fiesta
Suppliers: Yate

F1 Galia
Suppliers: T&M
Ha'on
Suppliers: Yate
Hero of Lockinge
Suppliers: Sutt
Honey Dew
Suppliers: Bakk
Jenny Lind
Suppliers: T&M
Minnesota Midget
Suppliers: T&M
Ogen
Suppliers: Barb; Brwn; Butc; CGar; D&D; Dob; EWK; John; JWB; Mars; Mole; Rog; Sutt; T&M; Toze; Tuck; VanH
F1 Overgen Panogen
Suppliers: Bree
F1 Romeo
Suppliers: Mars
F1 Summer Dream
Suppliers: Bakk
F1 Sweetheart
Suppliers: Barb; Brwn; Butc; Cart; CGar; D&D; Dob; EWK; Foth; John; JWB; Mars; Mole; OGC; Rog; Suff; Sutt; T&M; Tuck; Unwi; Yate

Synonyms

Westlandia Sugar see Honey Dew

Witte Suiker see Honey Dew

Melukhie
Corchorus olitorius
Melukhie
Not only is this plant an important source of Jute but it is also a vegetable much grown in eastern Mediterranean countries, much esteemed in Egypt. Melukhie is used in the same way as spinach, in chicken soups, as puree or with cheese and flavouring in strudel dough for a delicious pastry boreka. Although, being a native of hot countries, it will probably need a hot summer to succeed well in this country, it nevertheless should be worth a trial as a hlf-hardy annual. (Chil)

Suppliers: Chil

Mesclun
Mixed Salad Leaf
Suppliers: Foth

Mibuna Greens
Related to mizuna greens, but uncertain.

The latest escapee from behind the bamboo curtain. A Japanese vegetable with a long history of cultivation in Mibu near Kyoto. Joy Larkcom uses it in winter salads and stir fries, and says that most people like the taste very much.

Green Spray
Suppliers: Dob

Miner's Lettuce
Claytonia perfoliata

Also known as Winter Purslane, and sown in late summer for harvesting for salads through the winter.

Miner's Lettuce
Suppliers: CGar; Cham; Chil; D&D; EWK; OGC; Poyn; Suff; Sutt; Unwi

Mitsuba
Cryptotaenia japonica

Also known as Japanese Parley, this, like parsley, is a member of the Umbellifer family. Mitsuba is said to taste of celery, parley and angelica combined.

Mitsuba
Suppliers: CGar; CGar; D&D; EWK; OGC; Poyn; SbS; SMM

Mizuna Greens
Brassica rapa var. *nipposinica* or var. *japonica*

Related to Komatsuna, these exceptionally pretty plants can be used at any stage, from small seedlings to large plant.

Mizuna
Suppliers: CGar; Chil; D&D; EWK; Futu; OGC; SbS; SMM; Suff
Youzen
Suppliers: Dob

Mustard
Brasicca spp

Grown either as part of the traditional mustard and cress, or as a green manure.

    Black
        Suppliers: Cham
    Burgonde
        Suppliers: Suff
    Fine White
        Suppliers: Barb; Butc; Mars; SbS; Suff; Unwi
    Mustard
        Suppliers: Brwn; Foth; OGC
    Tilney
        Suppliers: CGar; EWK; Rog; Yate
    White
        Suppliers: Cart; Cham; Chil; Dob; John; JWB; Sutt; VanH

Mustard Greens
Brassica juncea

Another diverse group of oriental brasssicas, also known as Chinese mustard greens and Indian mustard greens. Gai Choy (Kaai tsoi) is the Cantonese for Mustard Green, and not a variety name, but until the seed suppliers start labelling their varieties properly it will be impossible to place their offerings into the correct group.

    Gai Choy
    Many suppliers call this Green in Snow, but strictly Green in Snow is one group of Mustard Greens, and Gai Choy is just another name for Mustard Greens. We need more information if we are to make use of these excellent vegetables.
        Suppliers: Butc; CGar; D&D; EWK; OGC; SbS; SMM; Suff; Sutt; T&M
    Kaai Tsoi
    Just another spelling of Gai Choy.
        Suppliers: Suff
    Red Mustard
        Suppliers: Futu

Mustard Greens (Broad Leaf)
var. *rugosa*
    Amsoi
        Suppliers: Suff

Oca
Oxalis tuberosa
    Oca
        Suppliers: Poyn
    Red Skinned
        Suppliers: Futu
    White Skinned
        Suppliers: Futu

Okra
Abelmoschus esculentus
Edible pods from a member of the Mallow family. Related to cotton.
    F1 Annie Oakley
        Suppliers: Suff
    Clemson's Spineless
        Suppliers: Chil; EWK; Foth; John; JWB; Mole; SbS; SMM; T&M
    Dwarf Green Longpod
        Suppliers: SbS
    Green Velvet
        Suppliers: Unwi
    Long Green
        Suppliers: Dob; Sutt
    Okra
        Suppliers: Bakk; CGar
    Pent Green
        Suppliers: SbS
    Perkin's Spineless
        Suppliers: Butc

Onion

Allium cepa

Agusta Rijnsburger
Suppliers: SbS

Ailsa Craig
An old, tried, tested and favourite variety, suitable for spring or autumn sowing, with large, globe-shaped, mild-flavoured bulbs with rich, straw-coloured skins. (Chil)
Suppliers: Bakk; Barb; Brwn; Butc; Cart; CGar; Chil; D&D; Dob; EWK; Foth; John; JWB; Mars; MAS; Mole; OGC; Rog; SbS; SMM; Sutt; Tuck; Unwi; VanH

Ailsa Craig Crosslings Seedling
Suppliers: Barb; EWK; Rog; VanH

F1 Alamo
Suppliers: Bree; Foth

F1 Albion
Suppliers: Bakk; John; Mars; T&M; VanH

Alix
Suppliers: Bree

Autumn Gold
Large, solid onions, half-round in shape. The attractive deep golden skins are really strong and the onions will keep until April or May from a September harvest. The crop is always huge and we have rarely known any bolters. (Mars)
Suppliers: Mars

Balstora
Balstora produces a very heavy crop of beautiful globe-shaped onions with golden-brown skins. You should expect it to store at least until early May (Mars)
Suppliers: Brwn; Dob; John; Mars; Mole; SbS; VanH; Yate

Barletta
Specially selected for pickling. Sow thickly in the rows in order to obtain beautiful, fine onions. One of the most popular silverskin onions. (Bakk)
Suppliers: Bakk; Mole; SbS; Suff

Beacon
Suppliers: SMM

Bedfordshire Champion
Good-sized globe. Long keeper, Improved strain. (Mars)
Suppliers: Barb; Brwn; Cart; CGar; Chil; D&D; Dob; EWK; Foth; John; JWB; Mars; MAS; Mole; OGC; Rog; SbS; SMM; Sutt; Unwi

Best Of All
Suppliers: SbS; Toze
Bola
Suppliers: SbS
Brown Skin
Suppliers: SbS
Brunswick
Flattish round, deep red onion with good keeping qualities. It has an excellent flavour and will give very high yields. (Bakk)
Suppliers: Bakk; Barb; EWK; Foth; Sutt
F1 Buffalo
Suppliers: CGar; Dob; Foth; JWB; MAS; Mole; SbS; T&M; Toze; Tuck
F1 Cadix
Suppliers: Bree
F1 Caribo
Suppliers: Bree; T&M
F1 Centurion
Suppliers: Dob; EWK; Rog; Unwi
F1 Dinaro
Suppliers: RSlu
Dobies' All Rounder
Round straw-coloured onions of fine flavour and of medium size—just right for the kitchen. Being quite thin necked, they keep extremely well in winter storage, remaining in good condition until February and March. Dutch grown. (Dob)
Suppliers: Dob
Downing Yellow Globe
Suppliers: SbS
Early Dirklander
Suppliers: SbS
Early Yellow Globe
Suppliers: SbS
Ebeneezer
Suppliers: SbS
F1 Express Harvest Yellow
Suppliers: Butc; CGar; EWK; JWB; Mole; OGC; Rog; SbS; Suff
Extra Early Kaizuka
Flattish bulb ripening to pale yellow. (Sutt)
Suppliers: CGar; D&D; EWK; Rog; Sutt

First Early

Onion sets for autumn sowing which produce a crop in June and July before the spring sown varieties have matured. With medium sized, flat bulbs of mild flavour, this variety is sown in September and will stand all but the most severe of weather conditions. (OGC)

Suppliers: OGC

Giant Fen Globe

Produce a huge crop of perfectly shaped onions, often 50lbs or more from each bag planted. In our trials they give a higher yield than any other onion. They will usually keep until late May and have a fairly mild taste. (Mars)

Suppliers: Mars

Giant Rocca Brown

Suppliers: SbS

Giant Rocca Lemon

Suppliers: SbS

Giant Zittau

Produces excellent medium-sized pickles, pale brown in colour. Sow in March. (Mars)

Suppliers: EWK; Mars; OGC; SbS; Toze

F1 Gion Festival

Suppliers: Yate

Golden Ball

A most receptive onion set because it loves to be planted late. At this time the weather is warmer. Hence it avoids some of the pitfalls earlier sets face. It is a very rapid grower and planted 6 weeks later will be ready at approximately the same time as regular varieties and has comparable yield and long storage qualities. (T&M)

Suppliers: T&M

F1 Goldito

Suppliers: RSlu

Guardsman

Suppliers: Dob; Mars; Toze

Hikari Bunching

A modern type of spring or bunching onion, Hikari is a versatile performer. From a spring sowing, it can be harvested over a long period as it does not form bulbs. Begin pulling at pencil thickness and continue through to the size of a small carrot. Distinctive, delicious taste. (Dob)

Suppliers: CGar; Dob; EWK; JWB; Mole; RSlu; SbS; SMM; Toze; Yate

F1 Hygro

Suppliers: Brwn; D&D; Dob; EWK; John; JWB; Mars; Mole; OGC; Rog; SbS; SMM; Toze; Tuck; Unwi; Yate

F1 Hyper
Suppliers: SbS
F1 Hysam
Suppliers: Brwn; Mole; SbS
F1 Hyton
Suppliers: SbS
Imai Early Yellow
Semi-globe shape, maturing from late June. Yellow skin. (Mars)
Suppliers: Mars; Mole; SbS; Yate
Indared
Suppliers: Yate
Ishiko Straight Leaf
Suppliers: Yate
Ishikura
A new bunching onion: a cross between leek and coarse chives. Ishikura is a fast grower. It has beautiful, fairly long, white stems, and dark green leaves. An extremely prolific variety. (Bakk)
Suppliers: Bakk; CGar; EWK; Foth; John; OGC; SbS; Sutt; T&M; Tuck
James Long Keeping
A good old variety with a very pleasant taste and first-class looks. The reddish brown, globe-shaped bulbs are excellent keepers. (Foth)
Suppliers: Barb; CGar; Foth; Rog; SbS; Suff; VanH
Jumbo
It has a golden-brown skin, is a perfect ball shape, large , solid and very uniform. One of the heaviest croppers, with exceptionally good keeping qualities. (Unwi)
Suppliers: Bree; Dob; SbS
F1 Karato
Suppliers: Bree
F1 Katisha
Suppliers: Yate
F1 Keepwell
Suppliers: T&M; Yate
Klabro
Suppliers: Sutt
Kyoto Market
Suppliers: Bree; SbS

Lancastrian
A giant globe shape variety ideal for exhibitions with sweet, crisp, white flesh and golden yellow skin. It is also excellent for cooking and storing. (Foth)
Suppliers: CGar; Foth; John; SMM; T&M

Long Red Florence
The traditional torpedo shaped red onion from Florence in Italy. Very reliable producing good sized bulbs with deep purple red colour. (Suff)
Suppliers: Suff

Long White Tokyo
Suppliers: Chil

F1 Mambo
Suppliers: Bree

Mammoth
Suppliers: CGar; JWB; Rob

Mammoth Red
Largest red onion in cultivation, has excellent keeping qualities with strong flavour. (CGar)
Suppliers: CGar; JWB; Rob

F1 Maraton
Suppliers: Bakk; Dob

F1 Mardito
Suppliers: RSlu

Monkston
Our new introduction which has been bred for exhibition use. Very large bulbs of superb shape and uniformity. (EWK)
Suppliers: CGar; EWK; JWB; Rog; SbS; SMM

Multi-stalk 5
Suppliers: Chil

New Brown Pickling
Suppliers: Mole; SbS

Nocera
Suppliers: SbS

F1 Norstar
Suppliers: Bakk; EWK; Yate

North Holland Blood Red
Large red-skinned globe with crisp, pink flesh throughout. Stores very well. (Foth)
Suppliers: John; T&M; Unwi

North Holland Blood Red Redmate
Suppliers: Sutt

North Holland Flat Yellow
Suppliers: SbS
Oporto
Suppliers: RSlu; SbS
Paris Silver Skin
Excellent 'cocktail' pickler. Sow March to late June, lift when about marble size. (Mars)
Suppliers: Barb; Brwn; CGar; EWK; Foth; John; JWB; Mars; OGC; Rog; SbS; Sutt; Tuck; Unwi; VanH
Pompei
Suppliers: SbS
Produrijn
Suppliers: SbS
F1 Puma
Suppliers: Dob
Purplette
The first ever purple-red skinned mini onion. Decorative and very tasty. The tiny bulbs turn a delicate pink when cooked or pickled. Can also be harvested very young as purple bunching onions. May also be left to harvest at normal size as mature onions. (Suff)
Suppliers: Mole; OGC; SMM; Suff
Radar
Suppliers: Mole
Red Baron
Early, prolific, flattish-round to round, deep red onion, suitable for eating fresh as well as for storing. Full-flavoured. Much in demand by the professional as well as by the amateur grower. (Bakk)
Suppliers: Bakk; Dob; JWB; T&M; VanH
Red Bunching Redbeard
A completely new bunching onion. Very decorative red stalks with colour extending in 2-4 layers. Extra decorative to use in salads. (Suff)
Suppliers: Suff
Red Delicious
Suppliers: Dob
Red Italian
Suppliers: SbS
Redmate
Suppliers: Yate

Reliance
A large, firm, flattish onion, it has a mild flavour and is a wonderful keeper. Recommended for spring sowing but can also be used for autumn sowings. (Unwi)

Suppliers: Barb; JWB; OGC; SbS; Suff; Unwi

Rijnsburger 4
Suppliers: CGar; EWK; Rog; SbS; SMM; Sutt; Toze

Rinaldo
Suppliers: SbS; Yate

Robot
A very good onion for storing. Brownish-yellow colour. Extremely high-yielding variety. Robot can deservedly be called one of the best selections. (Bakk)

Suppliers: Bakk

Robusta
Very heavy cropper with outstanding globe shape, fine quality skin and extremely long keeping ability. (EWK)

Suppliers: CGar; EWK; JWB; Mole; OGC; SbS

Rocardo
An excellent storing onion. Semi-globes with dark skins and a good flavour and texture. (Foth)

Suppliers: Foth; Sutt

Rocky
Suppliers: Yate

F1 Romeo
Suppliers: SbS

F1 Royal Oak
Suppliers: Foth; Toze

SY300
Suppliers: Yate

Santa Claus
Forms long stalks which do not bulb. Will hold well in the grounds without going tough and from approximately 8 weeks will start to flush red from the base upwards. A good flavour. (Foth)

Suppliers: Foth; T&M

Senshyu Semi-Globe
Like Imai Yellow, but maturing about 2 weeks later. Good sized solid bulbs. (Mars)

Suppliers: Barb; Brwn; Butc; CGar; D&D; EWK; Foth; John; JWB; Mars; Mole; OGC; Rog; SbS; Sutt; Toze; Tuck; Unwi; Yate

F1 Shakespeare
Suppliers: Yate

Showmaster
Developed from a top exhibition strain of onion, this special variety will produce the largest onions from onion sets. (Mars)
Suppliers: Mars

Southport Red Globe
A blood-red onion which grows to a large size, very popular with exhibitors and a change for the cook. A good keeper whose ancestors were grown for 17th centruy sailors. (OGC)
Suppliers: CGar; D&D; EWK; OGC; Rog; SbS; Suff; VanH

Sturon
A considerable improvement of the Stuttgart: extremely prolific globe onion. An excellent variety. Very much recommended! (Bakk)
Suppliers: Bakk; Barb; Bree; CGar; D&D; EWK; Rog; Tuck; Unwi

Stuttgart Giant
Flattish round onion which will keep for a fairly long time. However, the most important feature is that this variety can be harvested early. (Bakk)
Suppliers: Bakk; Barb; CGar; D&D; EWK; Mars; OGC; Rog; Tuck; Unwi

F1 Super Bear
Suppliers: EWK

F1 Sweet Sandwich
Suppliers: T&M

T 316
Suppliers: Bree

Tamrock
Suppliers: Yate

F1 Temple o' Gold
Suppliers: Yate

The Kelsae
Suppliers: CGar; JWB

The Queen
True silver skin. Sow thickly and the resultant competition will prevent the bulbs from getting too large for pickling purposes. (Dob)
Suppliers: Cart; Dob

Toro
Suppliers: Toze

F1 Toronto
Suppliers: Bree

Torpedo
Combining the flavour of a shallot with the sweetness of a Spanish onion is this most attractive-looking variety with smallish, red, torpedo-shaped bulbs. Thinly sliced, they add both savour and eye appeal to any salad. They can be sown in spring for a summer harvest or late summer for use the following year. (Chil)
 Suppliers: Chil
F1 Tough Ball
 Suppliers: Yate
Turbo
Exceptional onions which are vigorous, have high bolt resistance and store well. Very popular. (Foth)
 Suppliers: Barb; Bree; CGar; D&D; EWK; Foth; OGC; Rog; T&M; Tuck
Unwin's Exhibition
 Suppliers: Unwi
White Knight
There are usually few salad onions in June, because the overwintered crop has ended and spring sowings are not ready. It is possible to raise a fine crop of White Knight in this period by sowing in Propapacks in early February, transplanting outdoors in early April. Can also be sown outdoors from March onwards. (Mars)
 Suppliers: Mars
White Lisbon
A very popular salad onion with a particularly fine flavour for using fresh in various dishes and in salads. Pull the small white onions and cut off the top ends, leaving approx 20-25 cm. of the hollow leaves. (Bakk)
 Suppliers: Bakk; Barb; Bree; Brwn; Cart; CGar; Chil; D&D; Dob; EWK; Foth; John; JWB; Mars; Mole; OGC; Rog; RSlu; SbS; SMM; Suff; Sutt; T&M; Toze; Tuck; Unwi; VanH; Yate
White Portugal
 Suppliers: SbS
F1 White Spear
A bunching onion. Grows to a good size and has a very mild flavour. (JWB)
 Suppliers: Foth; Yate
White Sweet Spanish
 Suppliers: JWB; SbS; SbS
Wigbo
 Suppliers: SbS

Winter White Bunching
Stiffer, stronger foliage than White Lisbon. Can be pulled in May from an August or September sowing. Slower to bulb than other over-wintering salad onions. (Mars)
    Suppliers: Mars; T&M; Toze
Winter-over
Stands severe weather. Only suitable for autumn sowing. (Brwn)
    Suppliers: Barb; Bree; CGar; D&D; Dob; EWK; Foth; John; Mole; OGC; Rog; RSlu; SbS; SMM; Sutt; Unwi; Yate
Yellow Globe Danvers
    Suppliers: SbS
Synonyms
    Autumn Queen see Reliance
    Brunswick Red see Brunswick
    Brunswijker see Brunswick
    Crosslings Seedling see Ailsa Craig Crosslings Seedling
    Crosslings Seedling see Ailsa Craig
    Express Yellow see Express Harvest Yellow
    Giant Stuttgarter see Stuttgart Giant
    Golden Bear see Norstar
    Gros see White Lisbon
    Imai see Imai Early Yellow
    Imai Yellow see Imai Early Yellow
    Ishikura Bunching see Ishikura
    Ishikuro see Ishikura
    Kelsae see The Kelsae
    La Reine see The Queen
    Long White Ishikura see Ishikura
    Mammoth Improved see Mammoth
    Monkston Exhibition see Monkston
    Nordhollandse Bloedrode see North Holland Blood Red
    Oakey see Reliance
    Paris see Paris Silver Skin
    Red Brunswick see Brunswick
    Rouge d'Italie see Red Italian
    Senshyu see Senshyu Semi-Globe
    Senshyu Yellow see Senshyu Semi-Globe
    Stuttgarter Riesen see Stuttgart Giant
    The Sutton Globe see Bedfordshire Champion
    White Lisbon Winter Hardy see Winter-over
    Winter Standing see Winter-over

Zittauer Gelbe see Giant Zittau

Onion Other
Allium spp
Red Welsh Onion
  Suppliers: Poyn
Tree Onion
  Suppliers: Futu; Poyn; SMM
Welsh Onion
  Suppliers: CGar; D&D; Dob; EWK; Foth; Futu; Mars; Poyn; SMM; Unwi; VanH

Orache
Atriplex hortensis
Also known as Mountain Spinach, and long grown for its succulent leaves.
Garden Green
  Suppliers: Cham; Futu
Garden Red
  Suppliers: Cham; Futu

Pak Choi
Brassica rapa var. *chinensis*
Joy Larkcom is strict about reserving the name Pak Choi for this particular vegetable, and not confusing it with Headed Chinese Cabbage. There are many different types, each with different characteristics and uses, and in China the leaves are often dried in the sun for use in soups during winter.
F1 Joi Choi
A sturdy plant with wide, short leaf stalks that are white and flat. Very productive.
  Suppliers: Bree; John; Mars; OGC; SMM; Unwi; Yate
F1 Kaneko Cross
  Suppliers: Dob
F1 Mei Quing
The name means 'beautiful green,' referring to the green leaf stalks.
  Suppliers: T&M
Pak Choi
  Suppliers: Chil; Dob; EWK; JWB; SbS; SMM; Sutt

Tai-Sai
A soup-spoon variety, with elegant curved leaf stalks.
Suppliers: Bakk; CGar
White Celery Mustard
A soup-spoon type, with thinner leaf stalks.
Suppliers: OGC; SbS; SMM; Suff

Par-Cel
Par-Cel
Suppliers: T&M

Parsley
Petroselinum crispum
Berliner and Hamburg are grown for their roots, the others for their leaves.
Berliner
Suppliers: Bakk; Unwi
Bravour
Suppliers: Bakk; Brwn; Butc; CGar; EWK; Mole; Rog; SbS; Toze; Tuck; Unwi; Yate
Calito
Suppliers: Yate
Champion Moss Curled
Suppliers: John; Mole; OGC; SbS; Toze; Tuck; VanH
Clivi
Suppliers: T&M; Yate
Common
Suppliers: Bakk; Butc; EWK; Mars; Mole; OGC; Rog; Sutt; T&M
Consort
Suppliers: SbS
Curled
Suppliers: EWK; Poyn; Rog
Curlina
Suppliers: Cart; Dob; Foth; Mars; SbS; Unwi
Darki
Suppliers: EWK; SbS; Yate
Emperor
Suppliers: Toze
Envy
Suppliers: Dob; Sutt

Falco
Suppliers: John
French
Suppliers: Barb; CGar; D&D; John; Poyn; SbS
Frisco
Suppliers: Bree
Hamburg Omega Turnip Rooted
Suppliers: Dob
Hamburg Turnip Rooted
Suppliers: Butc; CGar; EWK; Foth; Futu; John; JWB; Mars; OGC; Rog; SbS; SMM; Suff; Sutt; VanH
Italian Giant
Suppliers: Poyn
Italian Plain Leaf
Suppliers: D&D; Yate
Moss Curled
Suppliers: Bakk; Butc; CGar; Foth; JWB; Toze
Moss Curled 2
Suppliers: Cart; Dob; Mars; Sutt
Moss Curled 2 Green Velvet
Suppliers: T&M
Moss Curled Afro
Suppliers: Bree; T&M
Moss Curled Extra Triple Curled
Suppliers: Barb; SbS; SMM
Moss Curled Krausa
Suppliers: John; VanH
New Dark Green
Suppliers: SbS
Omega
Suppliers: T&M
Paramount Imperial Curled
Suppliers: Sutt
Peerless
Suppliers: SbS
Regent
Suppliers: SbS
Robust
Suppliers: Toze

Thujade
    Suppliers: Bakk
Triplex
    Suppliers: RSlu
Verbo
    Suppliers: Brwn
Synonyms
    Gigante di Napoli see Italian Giant Leaved
    Halblange see Berliner
    Korte see Hamburg Turnip Rooted
    Mooskrause see Champion Moss Curled
    Mooskrause see Moss Curled
    Plain see Common
    Plain Leaved see Common
    Sheeps see Common

Parsnip

Pastinacea sativa
    Alba
        Suppliers: SbS; Toze
    Avonresister
        Suppliers: Barb; Brwn; Cart; CGar; D&D; EWK; Foth; John; Mars;
        MAS; Mole; OGC; Rog; SbS; T&M; Tuck; Unwi; VanH; Yate
    Bayonet
        Suppliers: Foth; Toze; Unwi
    Bedford Monarch
        Suppliers: SbS
    Cambridge Improved Marrow
        Suppliers: SbS
    Cobham Improved Marrow
        Suppliers: Cart; Dob; Mars; Toze
    Dobies Intermediate
        Suppliers: Dob
    Evesham
        Suppliers: SbS
    Exhibition
        Suppliers: Dob
    Exhibition Long
        Suppliers: CGar; JWB; Rob

Gigantic
Suppliers: T&M
F1 Gladiator
Suppliers: Bree; Brwn; Foth; Sutt; T&M; Toze
Harris Model
Suppliers: SbS
Hollow Crown
Suppliers: Bakk; Barb; Brwn; Cart; CGar; Chil; D&D; EWK; Foth; John; JWB; Mole; OGC; Rog; SbS; Tuck; VanH
Hollow Crown Improved
Suppliers: Dob; Sutt; Unwi
Imperial Crown
Suppliers: EWK; Rog; SbS
Improved Marrow
Suppliers: SbS; Yate
F1 Javelin
Suppliers: Foth; Toze
Lancer
Suppliers: Dob; T&M; Toze
Lisbonnais
Suppliers: JWB; Mole; SbS
New White Skin
Suppliers: Sutt
Offenham
Suppliers: Barb; EWK; JWB; Rog; SbS; VanH
Sydney Packer
Suppliers: Yate
Tender and True
Suppliers: Barb; Brwn; CGar; D&D; Dob; EWK; Foth; John; Mars; MAS; OGC; Rog; SbS; SMM; Suff; Sutt; T&M; Tuck
The Student
Suppliers: CGar; D&D; EWK; OGC; Rog; SbS; SMM
Viceroy
Suppliers: SbS
White Diamond
Suppliers: SbS
White Gem
Suppliers: Brwn; CGar; John; JWB; Mars; RSlu; SbS; Suff; Sutt; Tuck; Unwi; Yate

White King
　　Suppliers: Barb; D&D; EWK; OGC; Rog; SbS; VanH
White Spear
　　Suppliers: Bree; Toze
Yatesnip
　　Suppliers: Yate

Pea
Pisum sativum

Round peas are generally hardier than wrinkled peas, but not as tasty. Sugar peas are eaten pod and all.

American Wonder
A sweet, early pea. This much-prized variety can be grown without wire netting or twiggy sticks on humus-rich soils. It produces a heavy crop of long pods with very tasty peas. Ht 45cm. (Bakk)
　　Suppliers: Bakk
Ballado
　　Suppliers: Bree
Fonado
A very strong growing, widely adapted variety, will grow anywhere under range of conditions. Ht 100cm. (Bree)
　　Suppliers: Bree
Granada
　　Suppliers: RSlu
Masterfon
Marrowfat variety used for the production of dried peas. Ht 2ft. (JWB)
　　Suppliers: RSlu
Minnow
The first U.K.-bred, true Petit Pois Pea. Produces massive crops of narrow stump pods containing approximately 8 small, mid-green tasty peas. Ht 2ft. (Dob)
　　Suppliers: Dob
Petit Pois
　　Suppliers: D&D; EWK
Thomas Laxton
Early main crop, a good cropper with blunt-ended pods and sweet flavoured peas. Ht 3ft. (OGC)
　　Suppliers: SbS

Pea Round
Bountiful
A prolific, very early variety, highly valued by many, also by professional growers. This variety produces well-filled pods. Ht 140cm. (Bakk)
Suppliers: Bakk
Doublette
A very early, if not the earliest variety. Fine pea for preserving. Excellent quality and flavour. Dark green colour. Extraordinarily prolific. Ht 60cm. (Bakk)
Suppliers: Bakk
Douce Provence
Sweeter than Feltham First and just as hardy. Ht 2ft. (Mars)
Suppliers: Foth; JWB; Mars; Mole; Rog
Edelkrombek
Very popular, smooth-seeded variety (yellow-seeded). It produces tall plants, approx 140-160cm. in height, carrying lots of long pods, packed with delicious, juicy peas. (Bakk)
Suppliers: Bakk
Feltham Advance
Suppliers: Rog; SbS
Feltham First
An early, hardy variety with large, slightly curved painted pods. Ht 45cm. (Bree)
Suppliers: Barb; Bree; Brwn; Cart; CGar; D&D; Dob; EWK; Foth; John; JWB; Mars; MAS; Mole; OGC; Rog; SbS; SMM; Sutt; T&M; Toze; Tuck; Unwi; VanH; Yate
Fortune
Suppliers: Rog; SbS
Meteor
Very dwarf habit, ht 14in. (35cm). Small well filled pods. First early. (EWK)
Suppliers: Bakk; Barb; D&D; Dob; EWK; Foth; JWB; Mole; OGC; Rog; SbS; Suff; Sutt; Tuck; Unwi
Pilot
Very hardy variety for early Spring or Autumn sowing. Ht 36in. (90cm.). Long podded. First early. (EWK)
Suppliers: Barb; D&D; EWK; JWB; OGC; Rog; SbS
Prince Albert
An early, vigorously growing variety. This selection can be sown early. It will produce a bumper crop of yellowish-green peas. Ht 1m. (Bakk)
Suppliers: Bakk

Superb
Suppliers: JWB; SbS
Synonyms
Gladiator see Fillbasket
Petit Provencal see Meteor

Pea Sugar
Bamby
An improvement in Carouby de Mausanne, with the same very large flat pods but with a much improved, more compact plant habit. (Bree)
Suppliers: Bree
Carouby de Maussane
A truly magnificent mange-tout pea. Grow like a runner bean for a crop of flat thin pods that are unsurpassed for flavour. Attractive purple flowers. Ht 5ft. (Suff)
Suppliers: Bree; CGar; John; OGC; Rog; Suff
Delikett
Suppliers: RSlu
Edula
Suppliers: Unwi
Heraut
An early, heavy-cropping variety, very much in demand. It produces tender sugar peas, full of flavour. Should be trained upwards. Ht 140cm. (Bakk)
Suppliers: Bakk
Honey Pod
The earliest snap pea and indeed the sweetest. Producing smaller pods but many more of them than any other snap pea on a compact plant. They are also easier to harvest breaking cleanly without pulling the plant to pieces. (T&M)
Suppliers: Bree; T&M
Mange Tout
Eat all. (CGar)
Suppliers: CGar; VanH
Nofila
An outstanding early Sugar Pea with broad fleshy pods. Nofila has been bred to produce heavy crops on dwarf growing plants, ideally suited to the lack of space in modern gardens. Harvest the young pods whole and serve raw in salads or lightly cooked in other dishes. Ht 15in. (Dob)
Suppliers: Dob

Oregon Sugar Pod
Among the best of mange-tout with a particularly good flavour. Harvest while the pods are still flat and peas only just forming. (Foth)
> Suppliers: Bree; Cart; EWK; Foth; JWB; Mars; MAS; Sutt; T&M; Toze; Unwi; Yate

Reuzensuiker
Extra large, wide and fleshy pods, about 4in. long, produced on compact plants which need little support. Begin harvesting the pods as soon as they are large enough to pull and finish when the seeds inside start to swell. Very sweet. Ht 3ft. (Mars)
> Suppliers: John; Rog

Snowflake
More compact and later maturing variety than Oregon Sugar Pod with a similar medium long flat pod. (Bree)
> Suppliers: Bree

Sugar Ann
Very productive with big, fully edible pods on dwarf vines with juicy sweet flesh. Use fresh or cooked with or without the pods. (T&M)
> Suppliers: Foth; John; Rog; T&M; Toze; Tuck

Sugar Bon
An early maturing variety with medium length straw and medium-large pale green pods. Very easy to harvest. (Bree)
> Suppliers: Bree; Mars; Rog; Sutt

Sugar Dwarf De Grace
> Suppliers: Mole; Rog; RSlu

Sugar Dwarf Sweet Green
Yields a fine crop of sweetly flavoured pods. White flowers. Ht 3ft. (Dob)
> Suppliers: Bakk; Barb; Bree; Brwn; Chil; D&D; Dob; EWK; Mole; OGC; Rog; SbS; Suff; T&M; Toze; Tuck; Unwi

Sugar Lil
A main season variety with almost stringless large dark green pods on a vigorous plant. (Bree)
> Suppliers: Bree

Sugar Pod
> Suppliers: Bree

Sugar Rae
A late type to follow Sugar Lil with similar large dark green pods. (Bree)
> Suppliers: Brwn; Cart; Dob; OGC; Rog

Sugar Snap
Very long season of use. The pods are thick and fleshy and can be eaten as well as the peas—served together or separately. When young, the pods are

stringless. More mature pods can have the strings removed very easily. Very sweet. Ht 5ft. (Mars)

    Suppliers: Barb; CGar; Chil; D&D; EWK; Foth; JWB; Mars; OGC; Rog; SbS; SMM; Suff; Sutt; T&M; Tuck; VanH

Zuga

Mange tout, cooked whole when young. Ht 5ft. (JWB)

    Suppliers: Rog

Synonyms

    De Grace see Sugar Dwarf De Grace

    Norli see Sugar Dwarf Sweet Green

Pea Wrinkled

Alderman

Tall growing variety which needs support. Very heavy crops of long, well filled pods. Late maincrop. (EWK)

    Suppliers: CGar; D&D; Dob; EWK; Foth; John; JWB; OGC; Rog; SbS; Suff; Unwi; VanH

Almota

    Suppliers: RSlu

Avola

A vigorous grower in almost all kinds of weather. The peas have a dark green colour. They have an excellent flavour and lend themselves particularly well to deep-freezing. Ht 70cm. (Bakk)

    Suppliers: Bakk; Toze

Banff

A very vigorous early variety suitable for picking fresh and freezing. Three inch-long pods contain medium sized-peas of excellent flavour. Ht 2ft. (OGC)

    Suppliers: OGC; Rog

Bikini

The most widely grown semi-leafless type, with high yield and excellent processing quality, unique variety, semi-fasciated and highly concentrated pod set for maximum yield at freezing stage. (Bree)

    Suppliers: John; Rog

Cavalier

A heavy cropping variety, producing masses of pods, mostly in pairs, each containing 10-11 sweet, small peas. Very good resistance to mildew making it ideal for June-July sowings, in addition to main season. Ht 60-75cm. (2-2½ft). (Sutt)

    Suppliers: Brwn; Mars; Sutt; Toze

Coral
A high yielding early pea with a strongly determinate growth habit. Ht 60cm. (Bree)
Suppliers: Bree

Daisy
A short (2ft) main crop producing a heavy yield of excellent quality peas, 8-10 peas per pod. (OGC)
Suppliers: Foth; OGC; SbS

Darfon
Petit-pois. A new mid-late season variety producing a heavy pick of well filled pods giving an excellent yield of small dark-green peas. Its open habit helps to make picking easier. Ht 2-2½ft. (John)
Suppliers: John; Rog

Daybreak
Suppliers: Bakk; Bree; Foth; T&M

Early Onward
Heavy cropper, large blunt pods, ready 8-10 days ahead of Onward. Ht 60cm. (Bree)
Suppliers: Barb; Bree; Brwn; CGar; Chil; D&D; Dob; EWK; John; JWB; Mars; MAS; Mole; OGC; Rog; RSlu; SbS; Sutt; Toze; Tuck; Unwi; Yate

Ezetha's Krombek Blauwschok
The pods are bluish-violet in colour. The colour of the flowers is red. Ezetha can be sown for immediate use (at a young stage) as well as for drying (in which case they can be stored for used in the winter. Ht 180cm. (Bakk)
Suppliers: Bakk

Gradus
A second early variety ready in late June from an early April sowing. Good sweet flavour. Ht 4ft. (OGC)
Suppliers: Barb; CGar; EWK; John; JWB; OGC; Rog; SbS; Tuck

Holiday
Suppliers: Rog; Sutt

Hurst Beagle
Several days earlier than Kelvedon Wonder, this variety is truly sweet tasting. Blunt well-filled pods. Ht. 1½ft. (Mars)
Suppliers: Barb; EWK; Foth; JWB; Mars; Mole; Rog; SbS; Toze; Tuck; Unwi; VanH

Hurst Green Shaft
Carries a heavy crop of 4-4½in. pods of exhibition standard, which mature over a longer period than most varieties. Beautifully sweet peas. Ht 2½ft. (Mars)
> Suppliers: Barb; Brwn; Cart; CGar; Chil; D&D; Dob; EWK; Foth; John; JWB; Mars; Mole; OGC; Rog; SbS; SMM; Suff; Sutt; T&M; Toze; Tuck; Unwi; VanH

Jof
Tall late variety with plenty of vigour. Concentrated pod set at top of fine leaved plant. Ht 90cm. (Bree)
> Suppliers: Bree

Johnson's Freezer
This wrinkled seeded, maincrop variety is in great demand with food processors, being an excellent freezing variety. It is an abundant cropper, giving peas of excellent quality and flavour, the pods being borne in pairs on dark green vines. Ht 2ft. Not suitable for autumn sowing. (John)
> Suppliers: John; Rog

Kelvedon Triumph
> Suppliers: Rog; SbS

Kelvedon Wonder
An early variety with narrow tapering pointed pods. Suitable for freezing. Ht 45cm. (Bree)
> Suppliers: Bakk; Barb; Bree; Brwn; Cart; CGar; Chil; D&D; Dob; EWK; Foth; John; JWB; Mars; Mole; OGC; Rog; SbS; SMM; Sutt; T&M; Toze; Tuck; Unwi; VanH; Yate

Kodiak
> Suppliers: Brwn; Rog; Sutt

Lincoln
Very sweet flavoured peas. Heavy cropper, with dark green, curved pods. Ht 24in. (60cm.). Maincrop. (EWK)
> Suppliers: CGar; D&D; EWK; JWB; OGC; Rog; SbS; Tuck; VanH

Little Marvel
A proven sort, one of the most popular varieties. Ht 1½ft. (Mars)
> Suppliers: Barb; CGar; D&D; Dob; EWK; Foth; John; JWB; Mars; OGC; Rog; SbS; Sutt; T&M; Unwi; VanH

Lord Chancellor
A later maturing pea. Very heavy crop of dark green pointed pods. Very reliable. Ht 90-120cm. (3-4ft). (Sutt)
> Suppliers: Rog; SbS; Sutt

Markana
When grown in rows 6-12in. apart the extra tendrils of this sort help the strong-growing plant to support themselves without sticks and the seedlings are not attacked so frequently by birds. The numerous 3½-4in. pods are held in pairs, each containing 8-9 medium-sized, deep green peas with a good flavour. Ht 2ft. (Mars)
    Suppliers: D&D; Dob; EWK; Mars; OGC; Rog; Tuck; Yate
Miracle
Good quality peas on medium tall plants 4½ft (135cm.). Useful freezing variety. Second early. (EWK)
    Suppliers: EWK; JWB; Rog; SbS
Multistar
Uniform in growth with dark green sweet tasting peas. For best results this variety should be sown thinly. Excellent for freezing. Maincrop. (EWK)
    Suppliers: CGar; EWK; VanH
Nova
Earlier than Markana, this new many-tendrilled pea is superb for freezing. It is a reliable cropper, requires little or no support, and produces well-filled, dark green pods, each holding 7-8 delicious peas. Ht 2ft. (Mars)
    Suppliers: Mars
Onward
The main pea. Easy to pick. Ht 2½ft. (Mars)
    Suppliers: Barb; Bree; Brwn; Cart; CGar; Chil; D&D; Dob; EWK; Foth;
    John; JWB; Mars; MAS; Mole; OGC; Rog; RSlu; SbS; SMM; Sutt;
    T&M; Toze; Tuck; Unwi; VanH; Yate
Orcado
Main season variety with concentrated pod set at top of plant reducing harvest time and costs. Fine leaved. Ht 75cm. (Bree)
    Suppliers: Bree
Progress No. 9
Long podded variety with heavy yields of dark green, pointed pods. Ht 18in. (45cm.) Early. (EWK)
    Suppliers: Dob; EWK; JWB; Mole; Rog; SbS
Purple Podded
One of the few coloured varieties still in existence. Inside the very ornamental pods are sweet green peas of excellent flavour. (Foth)
    Suppliers: Sutt
Recette
    Suppliers: SbS

Senator
An exceptionally heavy cropper, ideal for the amateur gardener. The best main season variety. (Foth)
Suppliers: Bakk; Foth; Sutt

Show Perfection
Reliably produces an abundance of narrow pods about 6in. long and packed with round, dark green peas. Excellent flavour. (Dob)
Suppliers: CGar; Dob; JWB; Rob; Sutt

Trio
Three, four—even five-podded pea. Unlike other multi-podded varieties, the peas are of good size. Supreme for freezing, very sweet with an extra high sugar content and retained over a long cropping period. Invaluable if you are unable to harvest them immediately. (T&M)
Suppliers: T&M

Tristar
Mainly carried in clusters of 3, the blunt-ended pods, about 3in. long and tight packed with 7-9 sugary-tasting peas, are produced in profusion. Excellent when generous supplies are required for freezing. Ht 2½ft. (Dob)
Suppliers: Dob

Twiggy
An afila or leafless type, with large, easy to pick pods at the top of the plant. The leafless habit with intertwining tendrils means the plant stands up much better to the weather, making picking easier. Powdery mildew resistant. Ht 100cm. (Bree)
Suppliers: Bree; Foth; T&M

Uniroy
Suppliers: RSlu

Victory Freezer
Suppliers: Barb; SbS

Walton
Suppliers: Mole

Waverex
Produces a very heavy crop of blunt pods containing small, very sweet peas, sometimes called Petit Pois. Excellent for freezing. Ht 2½ft. (Mars)
Suppliers: CGar; Chil; Foth; JWB; Mars; OGC; Rog; SMM; Suff; Sutt; Tuck; Unwi

Synonyms
Chancelot see Lord Chancellor
Kelvedon Monarch see Victory Freezer
Laxton's Progress No. 9 see Progress No. 9
Telephone Nain see Daisy

Pepper Hot
Capsicum annuum
Hot and sweet peppers are botanically identical.
F1 Antler
  Suppliers: Yate
F1 Apache
  Suppliers: Brwn; Dob; John; Mole; Sutt
Cayenne
  Suppliers: Foth; John; JWB; Mole; SbS; Unwi
Cayenne Long Red
  Suppliers: Butc
Cayenne Long Slim
  Suppliers: Bakk
Chili
  Suppliers: CGar; D&D; EWK; OGC; Rog; Sutt
Crespin
  Suppliers: Suff
De Fresno Chili Grande
  Suppliers: Bree
Ethiopian
  Suppliers: Suff
F1 Hero
  Suppliers: T&M
Hot Mexican
  Suppliers: Mars
F1 Jalapa
  Suppliers: Yate
Jalapeno
  Suppliers: Foth; SbS
Karlo
  Suppliers: Suff
Magic Scarlet
  Suppliers: Bree
No Name
  Suppliers: Chil
Red Cherry
  Suppliers: Sutt
Serrano Chili
  Suppliers: Butc; Suff; T&M

F1 **Super Cayenne**
Suppliers: T&M

Pepper Sweet

F1 **Ace**
Suppliers: Mars; Unwi
F1 **Antaro**
Suppliers: D&D; EWK; Tuck; VanH
F1 **Ariane**
Suppliers: Bakk; CGar; EWK; Foth; John; Mole; VanH
F1 **Atol**
Suppliers: Bakk
F1 **Bell Boy**
Suppliers: Barb; Bree; Brwn; Butc; CGar; D&D; Dob; EWK; JWB; Mole;
OGC; Rog; RSlu; SbS; SMM; Toze; Tuck; Yate
F1 **Bendigo**
Suppliers: John; Mole; Toze; Yate
F1 **Big Bertha**
Suppliers: T&M
F1 **Blondy**
Suppliers: Bree
Bull Nose Red
Suppliers: SbS
California Wonder
Suppliers: Butc; Chil; Foth; John; Mars; Mole; SbS; Unwi
F1 **Canape**
Suppliers: Cart; Dob; SMM; T&M; Unwi
F1 **Carnival Mixed**
Suppliers: Mars
F1 **Clio**
Suppliers: Mars
F1 **Delphin**
Suppliers: Brwn; Mole; Toze; Yate
F1 **Eagle**
Suppliers: Brwn
F1 **Early Prolific**
Suppliers: Mars
F1 **Goldcrest**
Suppliers: Yate

Golden Bell
Suppliers: Butc; T&M
F1 Gypsy
Suppliers: Foth; Sutt; T&M
Hungarian Wax
Suppliers: OGC; SbS; Suff
F1 Jumbo
Suppliers: T&M
F1 Kendo
Suppliers: John
F1 Kerala
Suppliers: RSlu
F1 Leila
Suppliers: Bree
Long Red Marconi
Suppliers: EWK
F1 Luteus
Suppliers: Bakk; Brwn; Mole; Sutt
Marconi
Suppliers: Barb; CGar; D&D; Rog; SbS
F1 Mavras
Suppliers: Bakk; EWK; Foth; Mole
F1 Midnight Beauty
Suppliers: Sutt
F1 New Ace
Suppliers: Foth; John; Mole; OGC; SbS; Suff
F1 Panda
Suppliers: Bree
F1 Pantser
Suppliers: Bree
F1 Propa Rumba
Suppliers: Mole
F1 Queen Star
Suppliers: T&M
F1 Rainbow Mixed
Suppliers: Foth
F1 Redskin
Suppliers: Brwn; CGar; Dob; EWK; John; Mole; OGC; Sutt; T&M;
Unwi

F1 Redskin Dwarf
Suppliers: Foth
F1 Ringo
Suppliers: Suff
F1 Rubens
Suppliers: Suff
Salad Festival
Suppliers: Unwi
F1 Sirono
Suppliers: RSlu
F1 Slim Pim
Suppliers: SbS; Suff
Sunnybrook
Suppliers: Bakk
F1 Super Set
Suppliers: Bakk
Sweet Green
Suppliers: SbS
Sweet Spanish Mixed
Suppliers: Barb; CGar; D&D; Rog; SbS; VanH
F1 Tequila
Suppliers: Brwn
F1 Topboy
Suppliers: Suff
F1 Topgirl
Suppliers: Suff
Waxlights
Suppliers: Dob
Worldbeater
Suppliers: Sutt
Yellow Lantern
Suppliers: Dob
Yolo Wonder
Suppliers: OGC

Potato

Solanum tuberosum

Accent
First Early. 1991. Lifting just after Dunluce, in first trials it has produced shallow-eyed tubers which have been notable for their eating quality, with an excellent new potato flavour. The flesh is pale cream, waxy and firm after boiling. Accent continues to bulk up to produce a heavy crop and mature tubers show no cracking, even under drought conditions. (Mars)
Suppliers: Mars; Tuck

Adora
Early. A lovely early round white showing variety. (Scot)
Suppliers: Scot

Ailsa
Maincrop. 1894. Round oval, white, with cream-coloured flesh. Heavy yield of even tubers. Resistant to external damage, and highly resistant to blackleg. Susceptible to spraing and virus Y. (GPG)
Suppliers: McL; Rog; Scot; Webs

Alcmaria
First Early. 1969. Oval, yellow. Heavy early yield. Resistant to golden eelworm and slugs. Some resistance to common scab. (GPG)
Suppliers: Mart

Alhambra
Maincrop. 1986. Long, red, with waxy texture. High yield. Resistant to golden eelworm. Susceptible to leaf roll virus. (GPG)
Suppliers: McL; Scot

Alwara
Second Early. Red oval. Close waxy texture. Eelworm resistant. (Webs)
Suppliers: McL; Webs

Aminca
First Early. 1974. High yielding. (GPG)
Suppliers: McL; OGC; Scot; Webs

Antar
Suppliers: Scot

Arkula
First Early. 1982. Oval, white. Very high yielding early. Resistant to spraing. Susceptible to foliage and tuber blight, also blackleg. (GPG)
Suppliers: Mart; Scot; Webs

Arran Banner
Maincrop. 1927. White, round, with deep eyes. Heavy yield, but irregular shape and often hollow hearted. Susceptible to slugs. (GPG)
    Suppliers: Scot; Tuck; Webs
Arran Comet
First Early. 1956. Oval, white, with waxy texture. High early yield. Some resistance to common scab. Susceptible to virus Y, spraing, and blight, but is usually lifted before blight attacks. (GPG)
    Suppliers: Hend; Scot; Webs
Arran Consul
    Suppliers: McL; Scot; Webs
Arran Peak
    Suppliers: McL
Arran Pilot
First Early. 1930. Heavy crop early but matures too large with uneven tubers. Liable to fail from cut seed tubers. Resistant to common scab, drought, and spraing. Susceptible to external damage and virus Y. (GPG)
    Suppliers: Barb; Hend; Mart; Rog; Scot; Tuck; Webs
Arran Victory
Late Maincrop. 1918. Round, purple, with white, very floury flesh. Good cooking qualities. Heavy cropper that keeps well. Resistant to common scab. A favourite in Ireland where it thrives in the moist climate. (GPG)
    Suppliers: McL; Scot
Asparges
Early Maincrop. New salad potato, long tubers of regular shape with firm waxy texture. A first rank potato for the connoisseur. (Mars)
    Suppliers: Scot
Aura
    Suppliers: McL
Ausonia
Second Early. 1983. Round oval, white, with waxy flesh. Heavy early yield. Resistant to common scab, golden eelworm. (GPG)
    Suppliers: Scot; Webs
Avalanche
Second Early. Round oval, white, with white flesh. Very uniform tubers. (GPG)
    Suppliers: Scot; Webs
BF 15
    Suppliers: McL

Baillie
Second Early. 1981. Round, white, with shallow eyes. Moderate to high yield of uniform tubers. Resistant to blight. (GPG)
Suppliers: McL; Scot; Webs
Ballydoon
First Early. 1931. White, oval. (GPG)
Suppliers: McL
Balmoral
Suppliers: Webs
Belle de Fontenay
Early. For the very first salad potatoes. An extremely old French variety, which is still grown because of its exceptional culinary qualities. Small smooth kidney-shaped tubers with deep yellow flesh. Compact foliage. (Mars)
Suppliers: Mars; McL
Berber
Early Maincrop. White, round. High yield, stores well. A good all round variety, waxy. Eelworm resistant. (Webs)
Suppliers: McL; Scot; Webs
Berolina
Suppliers: McL
Bintje
Maincrop. 1910. Oval, white. Yellow flesh, high dry matter, resists drought, susceptible to blight and scab. Outclassed by Record, which is scab resisting. (GPG)
Suppliers: Bakk
Bishop
Suppliers: McL
Blue Catriona
Second Early. Long blue. Exhibition. (Webs)
Suppliers: McL
Bonnie Dundee
Suppliers: McL
British Queen
Second Early. 1894. Oval, white, with shallow eyes and white, floury flesh. Boils to mash if overcooked. Crops well. Resistant to slugs. Susceptible to blight and wart disease. (GPG)
Suppliers: McL; Scot; Webs
Bute Blue
Suppliers: McL

Cara
Late Maincrop. 1976. Oval, pink, with shallow eyes and floury, white flesh. Ideal for jacket baking. High yield of uniform tubers. Late foliage maturity. Like a better-tempered King Edward. Resistant to blight, golden eelworm and virus Y. Some resistance to blackleg. Susceptible to powdery scab, gangrene and slugs. (GPG)
Suppliers: Barb; Hend; Mars; Mart; McL; OGC; Rog; Scot; Tuck; Webs
Cardinal
Suppliers: McL
Carlingford
Second Early. 1982. Round oval, white. (GPG)
Suppliers: McL
Catriona
Second Early. 1920. Long oval, purple, with white, floury flesh. Low growing foliage which can be good for windy sites. Heavy cropper, haulm dies down early enough to miss blight and be lifted well before the worst slug attack. (GPG)
Suppliers: Hend; Mart; McL; Rog; Scot; Tuck; Webs
Champion
Suppliers: McL
Charlotte
Second Early. Developed in France during the 1980s to give tubers 50% bigger than other salad varieties. The crop is very uniform, shallow-eyed, long-oval in shape. The tender creamy-yellow flesh remains very firm and does not blacken on cooking. The excellent flavour—perhaps not quite as fine as Ratte—coupled with ease of culture ensures Charlotte's place in the first rank of potatoes for the connoisseur. (Mars)
Suppliers: Mars; Tuck
Civa
Suppliers: McL
Concorde
Suppliers: Mars; Mart; Scot; Tuck
Concurrent
First Early. White, oval, cream fleshed variety. Good drought resistance. (Scot)
Suppliers: Scot; Webs
Corine
Suppliers: McL
Cornes de Bique
Suppliers: McL

Costella
Second Early. Round oval, white, with yellow flesh. A good all round variety produces a heavy crop. Eelworm resistant. (Webs)
Suppliers: McL; Scot; Webs

Craigs Alliance
First early. 1948. Oval, white, with waxy flesh. Good cooking qualities. Moderate yield of uniform tubers. Susceptible to drought. (GPG)
Suppliers: Scot; Webs

Cromwell
Suppliers: McL

Cultra
Suppliers: Webs

Desiree
Maincrop. 1962. Long oval, red, with pale yellow, waxy flesh. Good for chips and baking. High yields but can get misshapen tubers on heavy soils. Crops well in drought, better than any other variety, even in 1976. Resistant to virus Y. Susceptible to mild mosaic virus, and very susceptible to common scab. Save your first lawn-mowings to put in the trenches against scab. (GPG)
Suppliers: Barb; Dob; Hend; Mart; OGC; Rog; Scot; Tuck; Webs

Di Vernon
First Early. 1922. Oval, white skin, purple eyes. A very heavy cropper and a good cooker, floury flesh. (GPG)
Suppliers: McL; Webs

Diamant
Maincrop. 1982. Oval, white, with non-floury texture. Resistant to blight. (GPG)
Suppliers: McL

Diana
Maincrop. 1982. Round oval, red. Heavy yield of large, uniform tubers. Early foliage maturity. Some resistance to blackleg. Susceptible to external damage and bruising. (GPG)
Suppliers: Scot; Webs

Doon Pearl
Suppliers: McL

Dr McIntosh
Maincrop. 1944. Long, white. Susceptible to blight and drought. Shallow eyes, slow in dry seasons, flavour only moderate. (GPG)
Suppliers: McL

Drayton
Maincrop. Oval, part-coloured, exhibition. (Scot)
Suppliers: Scot
Duke of York
First Early. 1891. Oval, white, with yellow floury flesh. Good for baking.
Moderate yields of small tubers but can be left to grow large for storing.
Susceptible to blight, wart disease and drought. (GPG)
Suppliers: Hend; Mart; McL; Rog; Scot; Tuck; Webs
Dunbar Standard
Late Maincrop. 1936. Long oval, white, with shallow eyes. Good keeper and
cooker, excellent for chips, but tendency to after-cooking blackening. Liable
to fail if tubers are cut. Late maturing, the haulm goes down in October.
(GPG)
Suppliers: McL; Scot; Tuck
Dunluce
First Early. 1976. Oval, white, with firm, cream flesh. Ideal for salad.
Perhaps the earliest early of all, good for greenhouse forcing. Susceptible to
blight and drought. (GPG)
Suppliers: Mars; Tuck
Edgecote Purple
Cropping unknown. A smooth skinned purple kidney with shallow eyes.
(Webs)
Suppliers: McL
Edzell Blue
Second Early. 1890. Round oval, purple blue, with white, floury flesh.
Knobbly tubers, excellent roasted or steamed. (GPG)
Suppliers: McL; Scot; Tuck
Epicure
First Early. 1897. Round, white, with deep eyes. High early yield. Tends to
fail from cut seed. Good frost resistance. Susceptible to blight and wart
disease. (GPG)
Suppliers: Hend; Mart; McL; Scot; Tuck; Webs
Estima
Second Early. 1937. Oval, white, with yellow, slightly waxy flesh. Good
cooking and keeping qualities. Heavy crop particularly at later lifts. Resistant
to blight, slugs and drought. Very susceptible to blackleg. Susceptible to
powdery scab, virus Y and spraing. (GPG)
Suppliers: Hend; Mart; Rog; Scot; Tuck; Webs
Etoile Du Nord
Suppliers: McL

Famosa
Suppliers: Webs
Fanfare
Early Maincrop. Round oval, pink. Exhibition. (Webs)
Suppliers: McL
Foremost
First Early. 1954. Oval, white with waxy, yellow flesh. Good cooker. Moderate yield. Poor foliage cover. Some slug resistance. (GPG)
Suppliers: Barb; Hend; Mars; Mart; Rog; Scot; Sutt; Tuck; Webs
Fortyfold
Suppliers: McL
Foxton
Maincrop. 1981. Oval, red-skin with light yellow flesh, firm floury texture. Excellent for roasting but some disintegration on boiling. (Seed)
Suppliers: McL
Fronika
Second Early. Round, red, waxy fleshed. Eelworm resistant. (Scot)
Suppliers: McL; Scot
Gladstone
Suppliers: McL
Golden Wonder
Late Maincrop. 1906. Long, russet, with floury, yellow flesh. Good baker, tends to disintegrate on boiling. Low yield of small tubers and does not thrive on all soils, suits the humid Irish climate best. Resistant to common scab. Susceptible toslug damage and drought. (GPG)
Suppliers: Hend; McL; Rog; Scot; Tuck; Webs
Home Guard
First Early. 1942. Oval, white, with waxy flesh. Prone to blackening after cooking. Sprouts fast and bulks early. Resistant to external damage. Susceptible to drought and blight. Picks up any taint such as BHC from the soil, an organic gardener's potato. (GPG)
Suppliers: Barb; Hend; Mart; Rog; Scot; Tuck; Webs
Jewel
Maincrop. 1985. Round, white, with non-floury texture. Heavy yield of large tubers. Does not discolour uncooked. Resistant to golden eelworm. Susceptible to gangrene and slug damage. (GPG)
Suppliers: Scot
Kennebec
Maincrop. 1963. Oval, white. Moderate to high yield, large tubers, close foliage cover. Susceptible to wart disease. (GPG)
Suppliers: Webs

Kepplestone Kidney
Early Maincrop. Round, pink. A top show variety in very short supply.
(Webs)
Suppliers: McL
Kerr's Pink
Late Maincrop. 1917. Round, pink, with floury, cream flesh. Ideal for chips
and does not blacken left cut up without water. Tendency to discolour and
disintegrate with boiling. A late maturing, high yielder with a compact
haulm that suppresses weeds. Quite susceptible to blight and scab. (GPG)
Suppliers: Hend; McL; Rog; Scot; Tuck; Webs
Kestrel
Suppliers: McL; Webs
King Edward
Maincrop. 1902. Long oval, pink and white, with floury, cream flesh. Good
jacket potato. Famous for yield and quality, but only on soils it suits. Needs
deep cultivation and was always a farm rather than a garden variety. Cut
seed often fails. Susceptible to blight, wart disease, virus Y and drought.
(GPG)
Suppliers: Hend; Mart; McL; Rog; Scot; Tuck; Webs
King George
Suppliers: McL
Kingston
Late Maincrop. 1981. Oval, white, with floury texture. Good jacket-baked.
High yielding. Golden eelworm resistant. Susceptible to blight. (GPG)
Suppliers: McL; Scot; Webs
Kipfler
Suppliers: McL
Kirsty
Maincrop. 1982. Round, white, with shallow eyes and creamy flesh.
Excellent for jacket baking and creaming. High yield, medium sized tubers.
Late foliage maturity. Some resistance to blackleg. Susceptible to spraing.
HDRA members report that this variety can be very susceptible to slug
damage. (GPG)
Suppliers: Mars; Scot; Tuck; Webs
Kondor
Maincrop. 1984. Oval, red, with yellow, creamy flesh that stays firm when
boiled. High yielding Dutch variety with very large tubers. Blight resistant.
(GPG)
Suppliers: Mars; Mart; Scot; Tuck; Webs

Lady Rosetta
Cropping unknown. Red round beautiful. With such a name it can only be an outright show-winner. A total beauty. (Scot)
　　Suppliers: Scot; Webs

Linzer Delikatess
Early. 1975. The soft yellow salad potato preferred by the Austrians. Bred in Linz in 1975, it has only just been registered for sale in Britain. It produces large numbers of medium-sized, long-oval potatoes, with superficial eyes. Delicious hot or cold. (Mars)
　　Suppliers: Mars

Liseta
Early Maincrop. Round oval, white. An excellent all round variety, bulks well to produce a heavy crop. Eelworm resistant. (Webs)
　　Suppliers: Scot; Webs

Lola
First Early. 1981. Long oval, white, with pale yellow waxy flesh. No discoloration. Earlier and heavier cropping than Maris Bard. Resistant to common scab and virus Y. Susceptible to tuber blight. (GPG)
　　Suppliers: Mars

Majestic
　　Suppliers: Barb; Hend; Mart; McL; Rog; Scot; Tuck; Webs

Manna
First Early. 1977. Oval, white, with shallow eyes and waxy flesh. Heavy early crop. Susceptible to blight and blackleg. (GPG)
　　Suppliers: Scot; Tuck

Marfona
Second Early. 1977. Round, white. Dutch variety, excellent for baking. Heavy yield, large tubers, good foliage cover. Good on light soils. Good overall disease resistance, including some to blackleg. (GPG)
　　Suppliers: Mars; Mart; McL; Scot; Tuck; Webs

Maris Bard
First Early. 1972. Long oval, white, with waxy flesh. Very early and high yielding, sprouts relatively late. Good forced under glass. Susceptible to powdery scab and blackleg. (GPG)
　　Suppliers: Barb; Dob; Hend; Mars; Mart; Rog; Scot; Tuck; Webs

Maris Peer
Second Early. 1962. Round oval, white, with waxy flesh. Moderate yield, plentiful small tubers, used for canned new potatoes. Early sprouter. Resistant to common scab and skin spot. Susceptible to drought. (GPG)
　　Suppliers: Hend; Mart; Scot; Tuck; Webs

Maris Piper
Maincrop. 1963. Oval, white, with floury flesh. Good baker. High yield, large number tubers per plant. Eelworm (golden) resistant and some resistance to blackleg. Susceptible to common and powdery scab, drought, and slugs. (GPG)
Suppliers: Barb; Dob; Hend; Mart; McL; Rog; Scot; Tuck; Webs
Mauve Queen
Suppliers: McL
May Queen
Suppliers: McL
Mona Lisa
Suppliers: McL
Mondial
Maincrop. Oval, white. Non-floury, stays firm when boiled and has a good taste. Produces a heavy crop. Eelworm resistant. (Webs)
Suppliers: Scot; Webs
Montana
Suppliers: McL
Morag
Early Maincrop. 1985. Oval, white. Moderate yield. Resistant to leaf roll virus. Partial resistance to both golden and pale eelworm. Susceptible to virus Y and tuber blight. (GPG)
Suppliers: Scot; Webs
Morene
Second Early. 1983. Round, white. High yield, large tubers. Resistant to common scab and golden eelworm. Susceptible to wart disease, gangrene and virus Y. Very susceptible to blackleg. (GPG)
Suppliers: McL; OGC; Scot; Webs
Nadine
Suppliers: Dob; Hend; Mars; Mart; McL; Rog; Scot; Tuck; Webs
Navan
Maincrop. Excellent white round-oval. Floury, firm flesh. Food for showing. Eelworm resistant.
Suppliers: Scot
Obelix
Early Maincrop. Yellow oval shallow-eyed variety with low dry matter. Suitable for exhibition. Eelworm resistant. (Scot)
Suppliers: Scot; Tuck
Palma
Suppliers: McL

Penta
Second Early. 1983. Round, pink-eyed, with yellow flesh. High yield, large tubers. Resistant to external damage. Susceptible to leaf roll virus, powdery scab. (GPG)
Suppliers: McL; Scot; Webs

Pentland Crown
Maincrop. 1958. Oval, white, with waxy flesh. Tendency to blackening after cooking. Very high yielder. Can be rather tasteless, but improves after Christmas. A supermarket suppliers' favourite. Resistant to common scab, leaf roll virus, virus Y. Some resistance to blackleg. Susceptible to slugs, powdery scab, spraing. (GPG)
Suppliers: Hend; Mart; Rog; Scot; Tuck; Webs

Pentland Dell
Late Maincrop. 1960. Long oval, white, with floury texture. Good for baking and roasting but tendency to blacken, and to disintegrate on boiling. High yielder. Very susceptible to tuber blight and spraing. (GPG)
Suppliers: Hend; Rog; Scot; Webs

Pentland Hawk
Maincrop. 1967. Oval, white, with waxy flesh. Good in salads. Moderate to high yields, long keeper. Susceptible to virus Y and spraing. (GPG)
Suppliers: Hend; Scot; Webs

Pentland Ivory
Maincrop. 1966. Round oval, white, with floury texture. High yield of large, shapely tubers. Some resistance to tuber blight and common scab. Resistant to virus Y. Susceptible to spraing. (GPG)
Suppliers: Hend; Scot; Webs

Pentland Javelin
First Early. 1968. Oval, white, with very white, waxy flesh. Slow sprouting, bulks late. Resistant to golden eelworm, virus Y and common scab. Susceptible to spraing. (GPG)
Suppliers: Barb; Hend; Mart; McL; Rog; Scot; Tuck; Webs

Pentland Lustre
Suppliers: Tuck; Webs

Pentland Squire
Maincrop. 1970. Oval, white. High yield of large tubers if on fertile soil. Prone to hollow heart, so needs high seed rate to prevent tubers getting too big. Some resistance to blight and blackleg. (GPG)
Suppliers: Hend; Rog; Scot; Webs

Pink Fir Apple
Late Maincrop. 1880. Long, pink, with yellow, waxy flesh. Salad potatoes, remaining firm when diced cold, appreciated in France where they make the real 'French Fried' Low yield, unusual shaped tubers. (GPG)
Suppliers: Barb; Hend; Mars; Mart; McL; Rog; Scot; SMM; Tuck; Webs
Premier
Suppliers: Barb; Mart; Scot; Tuck; Webs
Pride Of Bute
Suppliers: McL
Promesse
Suppliers: McL
Provost
First Early. 1981. Oval, white. Good foliage cover. (GPG)
Suppliers: McL; Scot
Purple Congo
Suppliers: McL
Ratte
Second Early. 1972. Long, white, with yellow, waxy flesh. Ideal for salad and boiling. Grown in France since 1972 as a higher yielding alternative to Pink Fir Apple. (GPG)
Suppliers: Mars; McL; Webs
Record
Maincrop. 1944. Oval, white, with yellow floury flesh. The highest dry matter potato, mainly grown on contract for potato crisps. Moderate to low yield. Resists blight, spraing and common scab. Susceptible to virus Y, blackleg, drought and internal bruising. (GPG)
Suppliers: Hend; McL; Scot; Webs
Red Cara
Late Maincrop. Round oval, red, waxy. Eelworm resistant. (Webs)
Suppliers: Scot; Webs
Red Craigs Royal
Second Early. 1957. Oval, pink, with shallow eyes and floury flesh. Excellent for potato salad, remaining firm when diced cold, as good as Pink Fir Apple, but a vastly greater yield. The only way to enjoy the old Craig's Royal flavour. Moderate yield, tubers large if left to grow. A good keeper. Resistant to powdery scab. Susceptible to external damage and hair cracking. (GPG)
Suppliers: Rog; Scot; Tuck; Webs

Red Duke of York
First Early. 1942. Oval, red, with floury flesh. Good for baking. The flavour, keeping and floury baking qualities of the old white skinned favourite, combined with good exhibition colour. (GPG)
Suppliers: Bakk; Hend; Mart; McL; Scot; Tuck; Webs
Red King Edward
Maincrop. 1916. Long oval, red, with floury texture. Good general cooking qualities. Moderate yield, large number of tubers per plant. Differs only in colour from the original. Resistant to common scab. Susceptible to wart disease, blight, virus Y and drought. (GPG)
Suppliers: McL; Scot
Red Pontiac
Maincrop. 1985. Round, red, with waxy flesh. Excellent jacket baked. An American variety. (Webs)
Suppliers: Scot; Webs
Red Stormont 480
Suppliers: McL
Rocket
Suppliers: Mars; Mart; McL; Scot; Tuck; Webs
Romano
Maincrop. 1978. Round oval, red. White flesh with a creamy texture. Stays firm on cooking. Moderate to high yields. Resistant to virus Y. Some resistance to blight and blackleg. Susceptible to leaf roll virus and drought. Like an earlier, less scab likely Desiree. (GPG)
Suppliers: Hend; Mars; Mart; Rog; Scot; Tuck; Webs
Royal Kidney
Second Early. 1899. Long oval, white, with yellow flesh. Keeps if left to grow large. Fine flavour. Susceptible to wart disease. (GPG)
Suppliers: McL; Scot; Webs
Russet Burbank
Suppliers: Scot
Russet Conference
Suppliers: McL
Ryecroft Purple
Suppliers: McL
Salad Blue
Second Early. Novelty blue flesh. (Webs)
Suppliers: McL
Salad Red
Suppliers: McL

Sante
Maincrop. 1983. Round oval, white, with shallow eyes and cream coloured, floury flesh. High yield of uniform tubers. Good all-round disease resistance, including resistance to golden eelworm, and partial resistance to pale eelworm. Some susceptibility to blackleg and gangrene. (GPG)
   Suppliers: Mars; Scot; Webs
Seaforde
   Suppliers: McL
Sharpe's Express
First Early. 1901. Long, white, with yellow, floury flesh. Ideal baker, but goes to mash if overcooked. Moderate to low yield, large number of tubers per plant. Keeps well. Like Duke of York, grown as an early for scraping and a second early for keeping. Susceptible to tuber blight and wart disease. (GPG)
   Suppliers: Barb; Hend; Mart; McL; Rog; Scot; Tuck; Webs
Sherine
   Suppliers: Scot
Shetland Black
   Suppliers: McL
Shula
Cropping unknown. Pink splashed oval white. Great for showing. Excellent long keeping firm fleshed variety. The best for baking or microwave use. (Scot)
   Suppliers: Scot; Webs
Spunta
   Suppliers: Scot; Webs
Stamina
   Suppliers: Webs
Stemster
Maincrop. 1986. Long oval, pink, with light yellow flesh. High yield, large tubers. Golden eelworm and slug resistant. Excellent exhibition. (GPG)
   Suppliers: Hend; Mart; Scot; Webs
Stormont Star
   Suppliers: McL
Stroma
Second Early. Oval, light yellow, with pale yellow flesh. Some slug resistance. (GPG)
   Suppliers: Hend; Mart; Rog; Scot; Sutt; Tuck; Webs
Ukama
   Suppliers: McL

Ulster Chieftain
First Early. 1938. Oval, white. An excellent early roaster. Has short haulm so does well on wind-swept sites and grows fast early, with a better crop than Arran Pilot by the end of June. Susceptible to blight, scab and frost damage. (GPG)
    Suppliers: Hend; Mart; Rog; Scot; Tuck; Webs
Ulster Classic
    Suppliers: McL
Ulster Prince
First Early. 1947. Long, white, with waxy flesh. Produces few tubers per plant. Emergence often slow and irregular. Forces well under glass. Resists drought. Susceptible to frost damage and very susceptible to spraing. (GPG)
    Suppliers: Rog; Scot; Tuck; Webs
Ulster Sceptre
First Early. 1964. Long, white. High yielder on fertile soil. Very early and high yielding, sprouts rapidly. Drought resistant. Poor virus resistance. Seed susceptible to mechanical damage and gangrene. (GPG)
    Suppliers: Barb; Rog; Scot; Tuck; Webs
Ulster Sovereign
    Suppliers: McL
Up-to-Date
Late Maincrop. 1894. Oval, white. Moderate yields, good keeper. Drought resistant. Susceptible to blight, common scab and wart disease. (GPG)
    Suppliers: McL; Scot; Webs
Urgenta
Early. Date unknown, pre 1981. Oval, red skin, yellow flesh, shallow eyes, heavy yields, excellent cooking quality and flavour. Dutch variety. (GSI)
    Suppliers: McL
Vanessa
    Suppliers: Hend; Mart; Scot
Waregem
Second Early. Oval, white with white flesh. Good for frying. Susceptible to slugs. (GPG)
    Suppliers: Scot
Wilja
Second Early. 1972. Long, white with yellow, waxy flesh. Good for potato salads. High yield with large number of tubers per plant. Blight resistant, and some resistance to common scab and blackleg. Susceptible to virus Y. (GPG)
    Suppliers: Barb; Dob; Hend; Mart; OGC; Rog; Scot; Tuck; Webs
Winston
    Suppliers: Mart; Webs

Witchhill
  Suppliers: McL
Synonyms
  Rode Eerstelling see Red Duke of York
  Sutton's Foremost see Foremost

Purslane
Portulaca spp
Grown for salad leaves in summer.
  Common
  Suppliers: Cham; Poyn
  Golden
  Suppliers: Suff; Sutt
  Green
  Suppliers: Bakk; Suff
  Yellow
  Suppliers: Cham

Radish
Raphanus sativus
Storage radishes, also known as winter radishes, have much larger roots that keep well.
  18 Day
  Suppliers: Suff
  Beacon
  Suppliers: SbS
  Bisai Japanese Seedling
  Suppliers: Suff
  F1 Briljant
  Suppliers: Mole
  Cello
  Suppliers: SbS
  F1 Cherokee
  Suppliers: Dob; John
  Cherry Belle
  Suppliers: Bakk; Bree; Brwn; CGar; D&D; Dob; EWK; Foth; JWB; Mars; Mole; OGC; Rog; SbS; Suff; T&M; Tuck; Unwi; VanH; Yate
  Crimson Giant
  Suppliers: SbS

Crystal Ball
  Suppliers: Sutt; Toze
F1 Cyros
  Suppliers: EWK; SbS; Yate
D'Avignon
  Suppliers: Suff
F1 Durabel
  Suppliers: Bakk
Easter Egg
  Suppliers: Suff
Fire Candle
  Suppliers: OGC
Flair
  Suppliers: John
F1 Fluo
  Suppliers: Foth
F1 Flyer
  Suppliers: SbS
Fota
  Suppliers: SbS
French Breakfast
  Suppliers: Bakk; Barb; Brwn; CGar; Chil; D&D; EWK; Foth; John; JWB; Mars; Mole; OGC; Rog; SbS; SMM; T&M; Toze; Tuck; Unwi; VanH
French Breakfast 3
  Suppliers: Cart; Dob; Sutt
French Breakfast Forcing
  Suppliers: Mole; SbS
French Breakfast Fusilier
  Suppliers: SbS; Yate
French Breakfast Lanquette
  Suppliers: RSlu
Gaudry
  Suppliers: Bakk
Globe Varieties Mixed
  Suppliers: Unwi
Helro
  Suppliers: John; SbS; Toze
F1 Juliette
  Suppliers: T&M

Karissima
Suppliers: Yate
Long White Icicle
Suppliers: Bakk; Barb; Brwn; CGar; D&D; Dob; EWK; Foth; John; JWB; Mars; Mole; OGC; Rog; SbS; Sutt; Tuck; Unwi; VanH
Novired
Suppliers: RSlu
Parat
Suppliers: Foth
Pink Beauty
Suppliers: Dob; John; Sutt
Poker
Suppliers: SbS
Pontvil
Suppliers: T&M
Prinz Rotin
Suppliers: Foth; Mars; SbS; T&M; Unwi
Revosa
Suppliers: VanH
Ribella
Suppliers: Mars
Riesenbutter
Suppliers: Bakk
F1 Rondar
Suppliers: Bree
Rota
Suppliers: Mole; OGC; SbS
Round Red Forcing
Suppliers: VanH
Round Red Forcing Real
Suppliers: SbS
Round Red Outdoor Gala
Suppliers: Bree
Rudi
Suppliers: Yate
Saxa
Suppliers: Bakk; JWB; Mole; SbS; Toze
Saxa Nova
Suppliers: Bree

Scarlet Globe
Suppliers: Bree; Cart; CGar; Chil; D&D; EWK; Foth; John; Mole; OGC; Rog; SbS; SMM; Sutt
Scharo
Suppliers: Mole
Short Top Forcing
Suppliers: Dob; Sutt
Sparkler 3
Suppliers: Barb; CGar; D&D; Dob; EWK; John; JWB; OGC; Rog; SbS; Sutt; VanH
F1 Speedar
Suppliers: Bree
F1 Standar
Suppliers: Bree
Summerred
Suppliers: RSlu
Volcano
Suppliers: CGar; EWK; Rog; SbS
White Turnip
Suppliers: SbS
Woods Frame
Suppliers: SbS
Synonyms
Flamboyant see French Breakfast
Ronde Rode see Round Red Forcing

Radish Storage
F1 April Cross
Suppliers: Bakk; Foth; Mars; T&M; Toze; Unwi; Yate
Black Spanish
Suppliers: CGar
Black Spanish Long
Suppliers: Bakk; Butc; Chil; EWK; OGC; SbS
Black Spanish Round
Suppliers: Brwn; Butc; D&D; Dob; EWK; JWB; OGC; Rog; SbS; Suff; Sutt; Tuck; VanH
China Rose
Suppliers: Barb; Butc; CGar; D&D; EWK; Foth; John; JWB; Mole; OGC; Rog; SbS; Suff; Sutt; Tuck; Unwi

F1 Easter
  Suppliers: Yate
Mino Early
  Suppliers: Dob; John; Sutt
F1 Minowase
  Suppliers: EWK; JWB; OGC; Suff; Tuck; Yate
F1 Minowase 2
  Suppliers: Butc; CGar
F1 Minowase No 1
  Suppliers: SbS
Minowase Summer
  Suppliers: D&D; Rog
Mooli
Not a variety name, but a general term for a long, white radish.
  Suppliers: EWK
Munchen Bier
  Suppliers: EWK; OGC; Suff
Ostergruss rosa
  Suppliers: Bakk
Red Flesh
  Suppliers: Suff
Rex
  Suppliers: Bakk
Robino
  Suppliers: SbS
F1 Silverstar
  Suppliers: Bakk
Tokanashi All Seasons
  Suppliers: Futu
Violet de Gournay
  Suppliers: Suff

Rampion

Campanula rapunculus

Although not widely grown, the roots of this biennial native plant are fleshy and good raw or cooked. The plot of the fairy story Rapunzel hangs on rampions being stolen from the magician's garden.

  Rampion
    Suppliers: Chil

Rape
Brassica napus
Usually grown as the cress in mustard and cress.
Broad Leaf Essex
Suppliers: Mole; SbS; Suff
Emerald
Suppliers: MAS
Giant English
Suppliers: JWB; MAS
Salad Rape
Suppliers: Brwn; Chil; EWK; OGC

Rhubarb
Rheum rhabarbarum
Early Red
Suppliers: Mars; Unwi
Glaskin's Perpetual
Suppliers: Butc; Chil; EWK; JWB; Mole; OGC; Rog; SbS; SMM; Suff; T&M; Tuck; VanH
Holstein Blood Red
Suppliers: Dob; SbS
Large Victoria
Suppliers: SbS
Prince Albert
Suppliers: SbS
Redstick
Suppliers: JWB; SbS
Strawberry
Suppliers: SbS
Timperley Early
Suppliers: Tuck
Victoria
Suppliers: Brwn; Butc; Foth; Mole; SbS; Sutt

Synonyms
Champagne Early see Early Red

Rock Samphire
Crithmum maritimum
Rock Samphire
Suppliers: Futu; Poyn

Rocket
Eruca sativa
Excellent in salads, it is doubtful that there are any true varieties.
Rocket
Suppliers: CGar; Chil; D&D; EWK; Futu; Poyn; Sutt
Rucola
Suppliers: OGC
Salad Rocket
Suppliers: Suff

Rocket Turkish
Bunias orientalis
Turkish Rocket
Suppliers: Futu

Rosette Pak Choi
Brassica rapa var. *rosularis*
Also known as Tatsoi and Tasai, this type of Pak Choi forms a flattened head, rather like an endive.
Tatsoi
This is not a true variety name, but simply the Japanese for Rosette Pak Choi.
Suppliers: D&D; Dob; EWK; OGC; SbS; SMM; Suff

Runner Bean
Phaseolus coccineus
Achievement
Outstanding variety for table or exhibition. Top quality and a long pod. (Mars)
Suppliers: Bree; John; Mars; Mole; Rog; RSlu; Sutt; Toze

Bokki
Straight, mid-green pods of good crisp texture and 10-11in. in length. (Dob)
Suppliers: Dob; Foth; Rog; Yate

Butler
This is a prolific cropper that is also completely stringless. Good sized tender pods on strong vigorous plants. Produces over a long period. (OGC)
Suppliers: CGar; EWK; OGC; Rog; Sutt

Crusader
A truly exhibitor's variety. Extra long, straight beans for home use or the show bench. (EWK)
Suppliers: Barb; Brwn; CGar; EWK; Foth; JWB; Rog; SMM; Unwi; VanH

Czar
A white seeded type with long rather rough pods. Good flavour cooked green, if left to dry will give a crop of butter beans. (OGC)
Suppliers: EWK; John; OGC; Rog; Suff; Tuck

Desiree
A white seeded variety that produces long slender, fleshy pods, at least 10in. in length. Exceptional flavour and stringless, it crops very heavily. 40 pods per plant can be expected. Suitable for freezing. (OGC)
Suppliers: Barb; CGar; D&D; EWK; Foth; JWB; Mars; OGC; Rog; SMM; T&M; VanH

Enorma
Very heavy cropper producing long, smooth, slender pods. Ideal for freezing. (EWK)
Suppliers: Barb; Bree; Brwn; CGar; Dob; EWK; Foth; Mars; MAS; Mole; Rog; RSlu; SbS; SMM; Sutt; T&M; Toze; Tuck; Yate

Fry Stringo
A white-seeded and white-flowering stringless runner bean. Nice straight long green pods. (Bree)
Suppliers: Bree

Gulliver
Tailor made for gardens where space is limited or too exposed to grow tall varieties. Outyields other low growing varieties and produces fine crops of slightly curved, smooth pods about 7in. long. These set early, are crisp, stringless and carried well above the soil. Plants usually reach a height of about 15in. If some long stems occur, simply pinch them back. (Dob)
Suppliers: Cart; Dob; Rog; T&M; Toze

Hammonds Dwarf Scarlet
A bush summer runner bean for the smaller garden, tops may need to be pinched out to stop running. Easy to pick and no poles needed. (OGC)
    Suppliers: Barb; CGar; D&D; EWK; JWB; OGC; Rog; SMM; T&M; Unwi; VanH
Ivanhoe
    Suppliers: Foth
Kelvedon Marvel
A selection from Kelvedon Wonder somewhat earlier in maturity. A heavy cropper it is deservedly popular with both gardeners and growers. (OGC)
    Suppliers: Bree; Brwn; CGar; D&D; EWK; JWB; Mars; Mole; OGC; Rog; RSlu; SbS; Toze; Unwi
Lady Di
Producing extra long slender pods with a smooth skin which are very slow to develop seed. (OGC)
    Suppliers: Brwn; CGar; D&D; EWK; Foth; John; OGC; Rog; T&M; Tuck; Unwi; VanH
Liberty
An outstanding variety for table or exhibition. Very smooth thick flesh with large number of beans per truss of great length many over 35in. (CGar)
    Suppliers: CGar; JWB; Rob
Mergoles
    Suppliers: Bakk; Dob; Foth; Sutt
Painted Lady
Add colour to the vegetable garden with the attractive red and white blossoms. (OGC)
    Suppliers: CGar; Dob; EWK; Foth; JWB; Mars; OGC; Rog; SMM; Suff; Tuck
Pickwick
A dwarf, bushy variety which does not need support. Ideal for starting early under cloches--which must be removed when the first flowers open. Even without protection, it is very early, producing lots of tender 8-10in. beans. (Mars)
    Suppliers: Foth; John; Mars; Sutt; Toze; Tuck; Unwi
Polestar
A select stock of scarlet-flowered runner, producing bunches of 10in. long stringless beans in profusion. It keeps its vigour throughout the season and the flowers set very easily. (Mars)
    Suppliers: Foth; John; Mars; Sutt; Toze; Unwi

Prizetaker
Outstanding quality. Good size pods useful for freezing. (EWK)
    Suppliers: Barb; EWK; Rog; SbS; T&M
Prizewinner
Excellent crops of good length beans. (EWK)
    Suppliers: Barb; Cart; CGar; Chil; EWK; JWB; MAS; Rog; SbS; Sutt;
    Tuck; Unwi; VanH
Red Knight
Red flowered, this crops very heavily and the stringless beans are excellent
for freezing. (OGC)
    Suppliers: Barb; Bree; Brwn; Cart; D&D; EWK; Foth; JWB; Mars; OGC;
    Rog; SMM; Suff; VanH
Royal Standard
Of vigorous growth. Produces many fine clusters of long, smooth, slender
slightly curved pods with a crispy rich flavour. Crops over a long period. Red
flowered. (Dob)
    Suppliers: Dob; T&M
Scarlet Emperor
Rich dark green pods frequently 15in. long. Preferred by many gardeners for
its flavour. (OGC)
    Suppliers: Barb; Cart; CGar; D&D; Dob; EWK; Foth; John; OGC; Rog;
    SbS; Sutt; T&M; Unwi; VanH
Streamline
Good pods of great length as well as texture and flavour. The shape and
uniformity of pods makes this useful for the exhibitor. (OGC)
    Suppliers: Bakk; Barb; Brwn; Cart; CGar; Chil; Dob; EWK; John; JWB;
    Mars; Mole; OGC; Rog; RSlu; SbS; Sutt; T&M; Toze; Tuck; Unwi;
    VanH; Yate
Sunset
    Suppliers: Sutt
White Achievement
White flowers, long, slender pods of fine flavour. Excellent for table and
exhibition. (Sutt)
    Suppliers: Sutt
White Emergo
Long slender pods with white beans. Good flavour and freezes well. (EWK)
    Suppliers: Bakk; Barb; Brwn; CGar; D&D; EWK; Foth; Mole; Rog; RSlu;
    SbS; Toze; Unwi; Yate
Synonyms
    Best of All see Streamline
    Emergo see White Emergo

Erecta see White Emergo
Goliath see Prizetaker
Kelvedon Wonder see Kelvedon Marvel

Salad Mallow
Malva crispa
Salad Mallow
A vigorous annual reaching 1m. and producing light green leaves with crinkled edges, and pale pink flowers, making it an attractive plant. The leaves are eaten in salads and have an excellent flavour and texture. Easily grown, with self-sown seedlings often surviving the winter. (Futu)
Suppliers: Futu

Salsify
Tragopogon porrifolium
Grown for its edible roots, which give it the name of Oyster Plant. It is doubtful that any of the varieties are truly distinct.
Giant
Suppliers: Sutt
Mammoth
Suppliers: Mars; Unwi
Salsify
Suppliers: CGar; Cham; Futu; Poyn
Sandwich Island
Suppliers: Barb; Butc; Chil; Dob; EWK; Foth; JWB; OGC; Rog; SbS; SMM; Suff; T&M; Tuck; VanH
Vegetable Oyster
Suppliers: John

Scorzonera
Scorzonera hispanica
Also known as Black Salsify, and also grown for the roots.
Black
Suppliers: Cham
Duplex
Suppliers: Bakk
Giant Rooted
Suppliers: SbS
Habil
Suppliers: Mars

Lange Jan
Suppliers: Dob; SbS; Unwi
Large Black
Suppliers: Chil
Long Black
Suppliers: Foth; JWB; SbS
Maxima
Suppliers: John; OGC; Rog; SbS; SMM
Russian Giant
Suppliers: Sutt
Scorzonera
Suppliers: Butc; D&D; EWK; Poyn; Suff; Tuck; VanH
Synonyms
Long John see Lange Jan

Seakale

Crambe maritima

A perennial that is not related to seakale beet. The blanched shoots make a delicious winter vegetable.
Seakale
Suppliers: Mars; OGC; Pask; Poyn

Shallot

Allium cepa var. *aggregatum*
Atlantic
Suppliers: Rog; Sutt; T&M; Unwi
Creation
Suppliers: Unwi
Delicato
Suppliers: Mars
Dobies' Longkeeping Yellow
Suppliers: Dob
Dutch Red
Suppliers: Barb; Rog
Dutch Yellow
Suppliers: OGC; Rog; Unwi
Exhibition
Suppliers: SMM
Giant Red Show
Suppliers: Scot

Giant Yellow
Suppliers: Mars; Sutt
Golden Gourmet
Suppliers: Barb; D&D; EWK; OGC; Rog; Suff; Tuck
Hative de Niort
Suppliers: Dob; JWB; Mars; Scot; Sutt
Pikant
Suppliers: Mars; Rog; Sutt; T&M
Sante
Suppliers: Dob; EWK; Rog
Sante Red
Suppliers: Tuck
Topper
Suppliers: Mars
Yellow
Suppliers: Bakk; CGar; EWK
Yellow Long Keeping
Suppliers: Foth

Skirret
Sium sisarum
The roots are cooked, like those of salsify and scorzonera. Could surely do with more selection to produce a fine vegetable.
Skirret
Suppliers: Cham; Futu; Poyn; Suff

Spinach
Spinacia oleracea **and others**
America
Suppliers: Yate
F1 Attica
Suppliers: Bree
Bazaroet
Suppliers: Bakk
Bergola
Suppliers: OGC
Bloomsdale
Suppliers: Barb; Chil; Mars; SbS
Broad Leaved Prickly
Suppliers: Bakk; Barb; Brwn; CGar; Chil; JWB; OGC; SbS; SMM; VanH

Broad Leaved Prickly Standwell
Suppliers: SbS
F1 Caballero
Suppliers: Unwi
F1 Carambole
Suppliers: Bree
F1 Correnta
Suppliers: RSlu
F1 Dash
Suppliers: SbS
Dominant
Suppliers: John; JWB; SbS; Toze
Eric
Suppliers: Bree
Fabris
Suppliers: SbS
F1 Galan
Suppliers: Bakk
Giant Winter
Suppliers: Bakk; Toze
Hollandia
Suppliers: SbS
King of Denmark
Suppliers: SbS
Long Standing
Suppliers: T&M
Longstanding Round
Suppliers: Sutt
F1 Mazurka
Suppliers: RSlu; SbS
Medania
Suppliers: Brwn; OGC; SbS; Suff; Toze; Unwi; Yate
F1 Melody
Suppliers: RSlu
Monarch Long Standing
Suppliers: Unwi
Monnopa
Suppliers: T&M

New Zealand
Suppliers: Bakk; Barb; Butc; Cart; CGar; Chil; D&D; Dob; EWK; John; JWB; OGC; Rog; SbS; Suff; Sutt
Nobel
Suppliers: SbS
Noorman
Suppliers: Bakk
Nores
Suppliers: SbS
Norvak
Suppliers: Dob; Mole; SbS; Tuck
F1 Novadane
Suppliers: Yate
F1 Oscar
Suppliers: SbS
F1 Parys
Suppliers: Toze
F1 Pavana
Suppliers: RSlu
F1 Polka
Suppliers: John; RSlu; SbS
F1 Predane
Suppliers: Yate
Prickly New Giant
Suppliers: Mole
Prickly Winter
Suppliers: D&D; EWK; Rog
F1 Rhythm
Suppliers: RSlu
Round Summer
Suppliers: CGar; D&D; EWK; Rog; VanH
Securo
Suppliers: Bakk
Sigmaleaf
Suppliers: Sutt
F1 Space
Suppliers: Foth; Mole
F1 Spartacus
Suppliers: SbS

F1 Sprint
   Suppliers: SbS
F1 Sputnik
   Suppliers: VanH
Strawberry
   Suppliers: Foth
F1 Symphony
   Suppliers: Mars
F1 Triade
   Suppliers: Cart; Foth
F1 Trias
   Suppliers: Bree
F1 Triathlon
   Suppliers: Mars
F1 Triton
   Suppliers: Sutt
F1 Valeta
   Suppliers: RSlu
Viking
   Suppliers: Foth; SbS
Virkade
   Suppliers: Toze
Viroflay
   Suppliers: Bakk; SbS
Viroflex
   Suppliers: RSlu
Wobli
   Suppliers: Mole; Toze
F1 Wolter
   Suppliers: Bree
Synonyms
   Giant Thick Leaved see Broad Leaved Prickly

Spinach Beet
Beta vulgaris
Also known as Chard and Seakale Beet; grown for the leaves and their fleshy midribs.
Erbette
   Suppliers: Suff

Fordhook Giant
  Suppliers: Barb; CGar; Chil; D&D; EWK; Mars; OGC; Rog; SbS; SMM;
  Toze; Tuck; Unwi
Italian
  Suppliers: Suff
Lily White Seakale Beet
  Suppliers: Barb; Chil; SbS; SMM; Suff; Sutt; T&M
Lucullus
  Suppliers: Bakk; SbS; T&M
Lyon
  Suppliers: Bakk
Perpetual Spinach
  Suppliers: Bakk; Barb; Bree; Brwn; Butc; Cart; CGar; Chil; Dob; EWK;
  Foth; John; JWB; Mars; Mole; OGC; SbS; SMM; Sutt; Toze; Tuck;
  Unwi; VanH; Yate
Rhubarb Chard
  Suppliers: Brwn; Butc; CGar; Chil; Dob; EWK; John; JWB; OGC; Rog;
  SbS; SMM; Suff; T&M; Tuck
Seakale Beet
  Suppliers: Barb; Butc; Cham; Dob; Foth; John; JWB; Mole; SbS; VanH
Synonyms
  Ruby Chard see Rhubarb Chard
  Silver Chard see Seakale Beet
  Swiss Chard see Fordhook Giant

Squash
Cucurbita spp.

The classification of squashes, pumpkins gourds, marrows, &c is
fraught with difficulties. Essentially, summer squashes are good fresh
and do not store long. Winter Squashes and pumpkins will store
well, particularly if allowed to cure at a good temperature.

F1 All Seasons
  Suppliers: Bree
Butternut
  Suppliers: EWK
F1 Cream of the Crop
  Suppliers: T&M
F1 Delica
  Suppliers: Mole; SbS; Toze; Yate

F1 Gourmet Globe
Suppliers: T&M
F1 Patty Pan
Suppliers: Bakk
F1 Sunburst
Suppliers: Bree; Suff
Vegetable Spaghetti
Suppliers: John; Suff; VanH

Squash Pumpkin
Atlantic Giant
Suppliers: Bakk; Foth; JWB; Mars; Sutt; Unwi
Autumn Gold
Suppliers: Sutt
Big Max
Suppliers: Bree
Big Moon
Suppliers: Yate
Connecticut Field
Suppliers: SbS; Suff
F1 Funny Face
Suppliers: Yate
Ghost Rider
Suppliers: Toze
Golden Hubbard
Suppliers: John; OGC; SbS; Sutt
Golden Nugget
Suppliers: OGC; SbS; Yate
Halloween
Suppliers: Brwn; Toze
Howden
Suppliers: Toze
Hundredweight
Suppliers: Butc; CGar; D&D; EWK; Rog; Sutt; Tuck; VanH
Jack Be Little
Suppliers: CGar; EWK; SbS; Suff; VanH
Jack O' Lantern
Suppliers: Bree; Butc; CGar; EWK; SbS
Jackpot
Suppliers: Unwi

Janne Gros de Paris
Suppliers: SbS
Large Yellow
Suppliers: SbS
Mammoth
Suppliers: Bakk; Barb; Brwn; CGar; Chil; Dob; Foth; John; JWB; Mars; Mole; OGC; RSlu; SbS; Unwi
Munchkin
Suppliers: Mole
F1 Nutty Delica
Suppliers: Bakk
Peelless Pumpkin
Suppliers: Chil
Pumpkin
Suppliers: SbS
Small Sugar
Suppliers: OGC; SbS; Toze; Yate
Spellbound
Suppliers: Toze
F1 Spirit
Suppliers: Yate
Sumo
Suppliers: Toze
Sweet Dumpling
Suppliers: Brwn; CGar; Chil; EWK; SbS; Suff; Toze
Sweet Mama
Suppliers: CGar; EWK; SbS
Titan
Suppliers: T&M
Triple Treat
Suppliers: Butc; SbS; Suff
Turk's Turban
Suppliers: CGar; EWK; OGC; SbS; Suff
Uchiki Kuri
Suppliers: CGar; EWK; OGC; SbS

Squash Summer
Cucurbita spp
F1 Tivoli
Suppliers: Dob; Mars; Mole; Sutt; Unwi; Yate; Yate

Squash Winter
Cucurbita spp.
Buttercup
Suppliers: Brwn; OGC; Suff; Toze
Butternut
Suppliers: Barb; CGar; Dob; Foth; SbS
Crown Prince
Suppliers: Toze
F1 Early Butternut
Suppliers: Yate
Gem
Suppliers: Toze
F1 Goldkeeper
Suppliers: Yate
Little Gem
Suppliers: Suff
Onion
Suppliers: Toze
Pompeon
Suppliers: OGC; Suff
Ponca
Suppliers: Toze
Red Kuri
Suppliers: Suff
F1 Table Ace
Suppliers: Brwn; Foth; Sutt; Toze; Yate

Swede
Brassica napus var. *napobrassica*
Yet another member of the cabbage family, grown for its enlarged root.
Acme
Suppliers: MAS; Mole; RSlu; SbS
Acme Garden Purple Top
Suppliers: CGar; Chil; D&D; EWK; OGC; Rog; SMM
Angela
Suppliers: Bree; RSlu; Yate

Best Of All
   Suppliers: Brwn; CGar; D&D; EWK; Foth; John; Mars; Mole; Rog; SbS;
   SMM; T&M; Unwi; VanH
Blauwkop
   Suppliers: VanH
Champion Purple Top
   Suppliers: SbS
Devon Champion
   Suppliers: Tuck
Laurentian
   Suppliers: Bree; RSlu; SbS; Yate
Lizzy
   Suppliers: Brwn; Cart; Dob; Foth; John
Magnificent
   Suppliers: Cart; MAS
Magres
   Suppliers: Bree; Toze
Marian
   Suppliers: Bree; Brwn; Cart; CGar; D&D; Dob; EWK; Foth; JWB; Mars;
   MAS; Mole; OGC; Rog; RSlu; SbS; Suff; Sutt; Toze; Tuck; Unwi;
   VanH; Yate
Peerless
   Suppliers: John; MAS; SbS
Ruta Otofte
   Suppliers: Bree; SMM
Western Perfection
   Suppliers: Sutt
Wilhemsburger Gelbe
   Suppliers: MAS; T&M

Sweetcorn

Zea mays

Should be planted in a block, not rows, to ensure good pollination.
   F1 Aztec
      Suppliers: John
   F1 BSS 3636
      Suppliers: Bree
   F1 Butterscotch
      Suppliers: T&M

F1 Candle
Suppliers: RSlu; Sutt
F1 Challenger
Suppliers: Toze
F1 Champ
Suppliers: Mars
F1 Citation
Suppliers: Toze
F1 Cobham Sweet
Suppliers: Toze
F1 Concorde
Suppliers: RSlu
F1 Conquest
Suppliers: T&M; Toze
F1 Dawn
Suppliers: Barb; CGar; EWK; OGC; Rog; SbS; Suff; Tuck
F1 Dickson
Suppliers: Bree; T&M
F1 Dynasty
Suppliers: Bree; T&M; Toze
F1 Earlibelle
Suppliers: SbS; Sutt; Toze
F1 Earliking
Suppliers: Brwn; Chil; Foth; Mole; OGC; SbS; Toze
F1 Earlivee
Suppliers: Toze
F1 Early Cup
Suppliers: SbS
F1 Early Pac
Suppliers: Toze
F1 Early Xtra Sweet
Suppliers: Unwi
F1 Excel
Suppliers: Bree
F1 Fiesta
Suppliers: Foth; Mole
F1 First Of All
Suppliers: Sutt
F1 Florida Stay Sweet
Suppliers: SbS

F1 GSS 3548
Suppliers: Bree
Golden Bantam
Suppliers: Mole; SbS
F1 Goldensweet
Suppliers: Yate
F1 Honeycomb
Suppliers: EWK; OGC; SbS; SMM; Suff
F1 Honeydew
Suppliers: Foth; JWB; SbS
F1 Honeysweet
Suppliers: Yate
F1 Indian Dawn
Suppliers: Toze
John Innes Hybrid
Suppliers: MAS
John Innes Hybrid Canada Cross
Suppliers: SbS
F1 Jubilee
Suppliers: Bree; John; Mole; SbS; Toze; Yate
Kelvedon Glory
Suppliers: Barb; D&D; EWK; Foth; MAS; Mole; OGC; Rog; SbS; Unwi
F1 Kelvedon Sweetheart
Suppliers: Butc; SbS
F1 Lariat
Suppliers: Toze
F1 Lumidor
Suppliers: RSlu
F1 Minor
Suppliers: Foth
F1 Miracle
Suppliers: Barb; Butc; EWK; Rog; SbS; VanH
F1 Morning Sun
Suppliers: D&D; EWK; OGC; Rog; SbS; Suff; VanH
F1 Northern Belle
Suppliers: EWK; Mole; SbS; Toze; Yate
F1 Northern Extra Sweet
Suppliers: Toze
F1 Northern Star
Suppliers: SbS

F1 October Gold
Suppliers: SbS
F1 Ovation
Suppliers: Toze
F1 Paris
Suppliers: Bree
F1 Peppy
Suppliers: Bakk
F1 Pilot
Suppliers: Bree
F1 Pinnacle
Suppliers: Toze
F1 Pioneer
Suppliers: Toze
F1 Reward
Suppliers: John; Mars
F1 Rosella 425
Suppliers: EWK
F1 Royal Crest
Suppliers: SbS
F1 Seneca Horizon
Suppliers: Toze
F1 Seneca Star
Suppliers: Toze
F1 Showcase
Suppliers: Bree
F1 Signet
Suppliers: Toze
F1 Snogold
Suppliers: Yate
F1 Snosweet
Suppliers: Yate
F1 Springsweet
Suppliers: Toze
F1 Sugar Boy
Suppliers: CGar; EWK; OGC; Rog; SbS; SMM; Tuck
F1 Sugar King
Suppliers: SbS
Summer Flavour
Suppliers: T&M

F1 Sundance
  Suppliers: Brwn; Dob; JWB; SbS; Sutt; Toze; Unwi
F1 Sunrise
  Suppliers: Cart; Dob; Mars; Toze
F1 Sweet 77
  Suppliers: Brwn; CGar; D&D; EWK; JWB; Mole; OGC; Rog; SbS; SMM; Suff; Toze; VanH
F1 Sweet Nugget
  Suppliers: SbS
F1 Sweet September
  Suppliers: Toze
F1 Tasty Sweet
  Suppliers: Bakk; EWK; SbS
F1 Trophy
  Suppliers: RSlu
F1 Two's Sweeter
  Suppliers: T&M
F1 Xtra Sweet Improved
  Suppliers: Mars
F1 Yukon
  Suppliers: EWK; SbS; SMM

Teff
Agrostis tef
A staple in Ethiopia, it may have something to offer gardeners in the U.K.
  Teff
    Suppliers: Futu

Texcel Greens
Brassica carinata
  Texcel Greens
    Suppliers: Brwn; Yate
Synonyms
  Ethiopian Rape see Texcel Greens

Tomatillo
Physalis ixocarpa
  Large Green
    Suppliers: Futu

Tomato
Lycopersicon lycopersicum
F1 1317
Suppliers: Yate
F1 936
Suppliers: Yate
F1 Abunda
Suppliers: Brwn; CGar; Mole
Ailsa Craig
Greenhouse/outdoor, cordon. Medium size fruit, very regular and perfect in shape. For real flavour, this is still one of the very best and it's a heavy cropper. (Unwi)
Suppliers: Barb; Bree; Brwn; CGar; Chil; D&D; Dob; EWK; Foth; John; JWB; Mars; Mole; OGC; Rog; SbS; SMM; Sutt; Toze; Unwi; VanH; Yate
F1 Alfresco
Suppliers: Brwn; Butc; Dob; JWB; Toze; Tuck
Alicante
Outdoor/greenhouse, cordon. An ideal variety for beginners, producing a heavy crop of high quality well flavoured fruit. (T&M)
Suppliers: Barb; Bree; Brwn; Butc; Cart; CGar; D&D; Dob; EWK; Foth; John; JWB; Mars; Mole; OGC; Rog; SbS; Sutt; T&M; Toze; Tuck; Unwi; VanH; Yate
F1 Allegro
Suppliers: Yate
F1 Angela
Suppliers: CGar; JWB; Mole
F1 Arasta
Suppliers: Barb; CGar; EWK; Mole; Rog; Tuck
Aurega
Dwarf variety for outdoors, fruit medium to small. (CGar)
Suppliers: EWK
F1 Beefmaster
Suppliers: Bakk; Barb; CGar; EWK; Rog; SbS; SMM; VanH
F1 Big Boy
Suppliers: Butc; CGar; Dob; EWK; Foth; JWB; Mars; Mole; OGC; Rog; SbS; Sutt; Tuck; Unwi; Yate
F1 Blizzard
Suppliers: CGar; Foth; Mole; T&M; Toze; Yate

Britains Breakfast
Lemon shaped fruit, red and very sweet, standard habit, has a very large spreading truss with many having over 60 fruits. Fruit does not split when ripe. (Rob)
    Suppliers: CGar; Rob
F1 Buffalo
    Suppliers: Bakk
F1 Calypso
    Suppliers: Mole; Toze
F1 Carmello
    Suppliers: Bree
F1 Cherry Belle
    Suppliers: Yate
F1 Cherry Wonder
    Suppliers: CGar; Dob; Foth; Yate
F1 Choice
    Suppliers: Bree
F1 Contessa
    Suppliers: Bakk
F1 Cossack
    Suppliers: CGar
F1 Counter
    Suppliers: CGar; Toze; Unwi
Craigella
Non greenback similar to Ailsa Craig. (CGar)
    Suppliers: CGar; EWK; SbS
F1 Cumulus
    Suppliers: Dob
F1 Curabel
    Suppliers: Butc; JWB
F1 Curato
    Suppliers: CGar
Currant
    Suppliers: Futu
F1 Cyclon
    Suppliers: CGar; Unwi; Yate
F1 Cyclone
    Suppliers: Brwn
F1 Danny
    Suppliers: CGar; John; JWB; Mole

F1 Dario
Suppliers: Mars
F1 Dombello
Suppliers: Dob; John; Mole; Yate
F1 Dombito
Suppliers: Brwn; JWB; Mars; T&M; Toze; Yate
Earliana
Suppliers: SbS
F1 Else
Suppliers: CGar
F1 Estrella
Suppliers: Bakk; Brwn; Dob
F1 Eurocross BB
Suppliers: Barb; CGar; EWK; John; JWB; Mole; Rog; Yate
F1 Extase
Suppliers: CGar; EWK; Rog
First In The Field
Very good for outdoor culture, vigorous growth. (CGar)
Suppliers: CGar; EWK; John; JWB; Mole; SbS
F1 French Cross
Suppliers: Sutt
Gardener's Delight
Small cherry-type fruit of outstanding flavour, ideal for salads and sandwiches, which can also be frozen complete. An exceptional cropper both outdoors and under glass. (OGC)
Suppliers: Barb; Bree; Brwn; Butc; Cart; CGar; Chil; D&D; Dob; EWK; Foth; John; JWB; Mars; Mole; OGC; Rog; SbS; Suff; Sutt; T&M; Toze; Tuck; Unwi; Yate
F1 Gemini
Suppliers: Dob
F1 Golden Boy
Suppliers: Sutt
Golden Nugget
Suppliers: T&M
Golden Sunrise
For those who like a little variation in their tomatoes. As the name indicates this is golden yellow in colour, medium in size, round, thin skinned, excellent flavour and a heavy cropper. (OGC)
Suppliers: Brwn; CGar; Chil; D&D; Dob; EWK; Foth; John; JWB; Mole; OGC; Rog; SbS; Sutt; T&M; Tuck

F1 Golden Tomboy
Suppliers: CGar; SbS
F1 Goldstar
Suppliers: CGar; Mole
F1 Grenadier
Suppliers: Barb; Butc; CGar; EWK; Rog; Sutt
Harbinger
An old favourite from the beginning of the century when tomatoes had flavour! A good tall outdoor variety or for growing under plastic. Thin skinned medium size fruit which will ripen well off the plant. (Suff)
Suppliers: CGar; Dob; EWK; JWB; OGC; SbS; Suff; Sutt; Toze
Heinz
Suppliers: SbS
Histon Early
Outdoor, cordon. A heavy cropper with bright red fruit of good size and quality and fine flavour. (Unwi)
Suppliers: Unwi
F1 Holland Brid
Suppliers: CGar
F1 Husky Gold
Suppliers: T&M
Ida
An early ripening and productive variety, particularly useful for growing in a cold greenhouse. Compact plant habit and close jointed with fruits of medium size. Cordon. Resistant to TMV, leaf mould, verticillium and fusarium. (Sutt)
Suppliers: Sutt
Ida Gold
Especially developed for cold climates. Forms a low branching bush producing masses of bright carrot-orange round super flavoured fruit of approx 2oz. Very colourful in salads and earlier than regular tomatoes. Outdoor or protected crop. (Suff)
Suppliers: Suff
Jubilee
Suppliers: Rob
F1 Kon Tiki
Suppliers: John
Kondine Red
Deep scarlet fruit on large trusses, heavy cropper. (CGar)
Suppliers: CGar

F1 Liberto
Suppliers: CGar
F1 Libra
Suppliers: Brwn
F1 MM
Suppliers: CGar
Magnum
Dutch early variety, non greenback, cladosporium resistance, A. B. resistance. (CGar)
Suppliers: T&M
F1 Manhattan
Suppliers: Bree
Marglobe
Large red fruit, thick meaty flesh of excellent flavour can be grown to over 1lb each tomato. (Rob)
Suppliers: CGar; Rob; SbS
Marmande Super
Outdoor only, semi determinate. Super Marmande has the sugar flavour of the old south European type combined with vigour. (T&M)
Suppliers: Bakk; Barb; Butc; CGar; Dob; EWK; Foth; JWB; Mars; Mole; OGC; Rog; SbS; SbS; Suff; Sutt; T&M; Unwi
F1 Master
Suppliers: Bakk
F1 Matador
Suppliers: CGar; T&M; Yate
Minibel
Tasty bite-size tomatoes can be grown in pots on the patio, in window boxes or on your windowsill, novel, miniature bush variety. (Foth)
Suppliers: Foth; Mars
F1 Mirabell
Suppliers: Foth; Mars
Moneycross
Greenhouse, cordon. An improvement on the popular Moneymaker variety being a heavy cropper of non greenback fruit. (John)
Suppliers: Barb; CGar; John; JWB; Mole; SbS; VanH
Moneymaker
Outdoor/greenhouse, cordon. Very reliable variety which has stood the test of time. (T&M)
Suppliers: Bree; Brwn; Cart; CGar; Chil; Dob; EWK; Foth; John; Mole; Rog; SbS; SMM; Sutt; T&M; Toze; Tuck; Unwi; VanH; Yate

Moneymaker Dutch Victory
    Suppliers: Toze
Moneymaker Stonor
A very heavy cropper, with fruits of medium size, bright scarlet in colour.
(Barb)
    Suppliers: Barb; CGar; JWB
Montfavet 63-4
A so-called bush type tomato, early maturing and fleshy, with a beautiful
round shape. Resistant to 'bursting', and, therefore, a sure cropper. Very
suitable for early cultivation under glass. Perfectly suited for making tomato
juice and ketchup. (Bakk)
    Suppliers: Bakk
F1 Monza
    Suppliers: CGar; EWK
Nepal
Big and exceptionally flowerful beefsteak type. Huge crop produced on a
vigorous vine with average weight of fruit 10-12oz. and some over 1lb. Our
favourite large tomato for slicing. Said to have originally come from Nepal.
Try it!(Suff)
    Suppliers: Suff
F1 Nimbus
    Suppliers: Sutt
Nova
Excellent paste or bottling variety. Enormous crop and early as well. Fruit are
elongated, red and 2oz in weight with little juice. Forms a low sprawling
bush so straw round it well. Outdoor or greenhouse culture. (Suff)
    Suppliers: Suff
F1 Ostona
    Suppliers: Yate
Outdoor Girl
This variety has been developed for outdoor cultivation, and its
characteristics include extreme earliness, large trusses bearing many medium
sized fruit, excellent flavour, a good red colour and sturdy plants. An ideal
outdoor garden variety. (John)
    Suppliers: CGar; D&D; EWK; John; JWB; Mars; Mole; OGC; Rog; SbS
Oxheart
    Suppliers: SbS; Suff
F1 Pannovy
    Suppliers: Bree
F1 Patio
    Suppliers: Bakk

F1 Phyra
Suppliers: CGar; EWK; Foth; OGC; Tuck
F1 Pipo
Suppliers: CGar
F1 Piranto
Suppliers: Mars
F1 Pixie
Suppliers: CGar; D&D; EWK; John; JWB; Mole; OGC; Rog; SbS; SMM; Suff; Sutt
Plumito
Smooth straight sided red fruit, sweet and fleshy, ideal for freezer or bottling, standard habit. (Rob)
Suppliers: Rob
Plumpton King
Popular red English greenback variety, unsurpassable for quality. (CGar)
Suppliers: CGar
F1 Prelude
Suppliers: Yate
F1 Primato
Suppliers: Bree; Dob
F1 Prisca
Suppliers: Mars
Red Alert
Outdoor/greenhouse, bush. Small fruits roughly 1oz each with a good flavour. Easy. No side shooting or training. (T&M)
Suppliers: Bakk; Brwn; Butc; Cart; CGar; D&D; Dob; EWK; Foth; John; JWB; Mars; Mole; OGC; Rog; Unwi
Red Cherry
Cherry sized fruit, good flavour, standard habit with long strings of fruit. (Rob)
Suppliers: Rob
Roma VF
Outdoor, bush. Continental type bearing brightly coloured long, fleshy fruits. Heavy cropping, and resistant to fusarium wilt. (Sutt)
Suppliers: CGar; Foth; Mars; SbS; T&M
Round Yellow Sunrise
Notably sweeter in flavour than most red tomatoes, standard habit. (Rob)
Suppliers: Rob
Rutgers
Suppliers: SbS

San Marzano 2
A typical 'Italian' tomato, producing longish, firm fruit. Extremely suitable for making the sauce that goes with spaghetti Bolognese, for tomato soup or for garnishing your salads. It gives a high yield of egg-shaped, firm-fleshed fruit. (Bakk)
> Suppliers: Bakk; Barb; CGar; D&D; EWK; JWB; OGC; Rog; SbS; SMM; VanH

F1 Shirley
> Suppliers: Barb; Brwn; Butc; Cart; CGar; D&D; EWK; Foth; John; JWB; Mars; Mole; OGC; Rog; Sutt; T&M; Toze; Tuck; Unwi; VanH; Yate

F1 Sigmabush
> Suppliers: Sutt

F1 Sioux
> Suppliers: Unwi

F1 Sleaford Abundance
> Suppliers: CGar; JWB; Mars; Suff

F1 Sonatine
> Suppliers: JWB; Sutt

F1 Spartan
> Suppliers: Dob

F1 Spectra
> Suppliers: CGar

Stonor Exhibition
Medium early, round red fruit excellent for the show bench, has the good old fashioned taste. (Rob)
> Suppliers: JWB; Rob

Sub Arctic Plenty
> Suppliers: CGar

F1 Sungold
> Suppliers: T&M

F1 Supersteak
> Suppliers: T&M

F1 Sweet 100
> Suppliers: Bakk; Bree; Butc; CGar; EWK; Foth; John; Mole; OGC; SbS; SMM; Sutt; T&M; Unwi

Sweet Chelsea
> Suppliers: CGar

F1 Sweet Cherry
> Suppliers: Foth

F1 Sweet Susan
> Suppliers: CGar

Tangella
Medium sized pale orange fruits of excellent flavour. Early ripening. Cordon. (Butc)
Suppliers: Butc; SbS

The Amateur
Outdoor. A very popular bush tomato. Good yield and quality. (Unwi)
Suppliers: Barb; Cart; CGar; Chil; D&D; Dob; EWK; Foth; JWB; Mars; Mole; OGC; Rog; SbS; Sutt; Unwi; VanH

Tigerella
Outdoor/greenhouse, determinate. Nearly seedless, plum shaped fruits with a pleasingly different flavour. (T&M)
Suppliers: Barb; Butc; CGar; EWK; Foth; OGC; Rog; SbS; Suff; Sutt; T&M

Tiny Tim
The ultimate in compact tomato plants. Perfect for pot or window box growing. Superb flavoured cherry sized fruit which are quite delicious whole in salads. (Suff)
Suppliers: CGar; EWK; Foth; Rog; SbS; Suff; Sutt; VanH

F1 Tomboy
Suppliers: CGar; D&D; EWK; SbS

F1 Tomboy Golden
Suppliers: EWK

F1 Tornado
Suppliers: Foth; Mars; Mole; Sutt

F1 Totem
Suppliers: Butc; CGar; Dob; EWK; John; Mole; Rog; SMM; Sutt; Unwi

F1 Tumbler
Suppliers: Brwn; Cart; CGar; Dob; John; Mole; Sutt; T&M; Yate

F1 Turbo
Suppliers: CGar; Mole; Toze

F1 Typhoon
Suppliers: Brwn; Dob

Whippersnapper
This must be the earliest tomato. You will be amazed how early and how prolific this variety is. Tiny (1in. long) oval pink fruits of a fine flavour. The plant has a sprawling or hanging habit compact and very decorative in a pot or hanging basket. Very little leaf. (Suff)
Suppliers: Suff

Yellow Canary
Suppliers: Mole

Yellow Currant
Small fruit, grape-like in appearance, long strings of tomatoes. Can be grown as a standard type in a pot or as a bush habit. (Rob)
    Suppliers: CGar; Rob
Yellow Pearshaped
Pear shape fruit, very sweet and solid with few seeds, standard habit. (Rob)
    Suppliers: Bakk; CGar; Rob
Yellow Perfection
The earliest and most prolific tall yellow tomato in existence. Recommended for outdoors. Cordon. (Unwi)
    Suppliers: Mars; Unwi
F1 Zorro
    Suppliers: CGar; EWK
Synonyms
    Freude see Gardener's Delight
    Marmande hative see Marmande Super

Tree Tomato
Cyphomandra betacea
    Tree Tomato
        Suppliers: Bakk

Turnip
Brassica rapa var. *rapa*
    Arcoat
        Suppliers: Yate
    Champion Green Top Yellow
        Suppliers: Tuck
    Early Green Top Stone
        Suppliers: Barb
    Early Snowball
        Suppliers: Barb; Foth; Suff
    Frisia
        Suppliers: Bree; MAS
    Gilfeather
        Suppliers: T&M
    Goldana
        Suppliers: Bakk

Golden Ball
Suppliers: Brwn; Cart; CGar; D&D; Dob; EWK; Foth; John; JWB; Mars; Mole; OGC; SbS; Sutt; Tuck; Unwi; VanH

Green Top
Suppliers: SbS

F1 Hakutaka
Suppliers: Dob

Imperial Green Globe
Suppliers: Sutt

Improved Purple Garden Swede
Suppliers: Barb

Manchester Market
Suppliers: Bree; Brwn; CGar; D&D; EWK; John; JWB; Mars; Mole; RSlu; Toze; Yate

F1 Market Express
Suppliers: Yate

Milan Early White Top
Suppliers: JWB

Milan Purple Top Forcing
Suppliers: Bakk; Bree; RSlu; Toze

Milan White
Suppliers: Bree; Dob; EWK; SbS; SMM; Toze; VanH

Milan White Forcing
Suppliers: Mars

Presto
Suppliers: Chil

Purple Top Milan
Suppliers: Brwn; Cart; CGar; Dob; EWK; Foth; John; Mole; SbS; SMM; Sutt; Tuck; Unwi

Purple Top White Globe
Suppliers: Bakk; Bree; EWK; SbS; Sutt; VanH

Red Milan
Suppliers: SbS

Snowball
Suppliers: Barb; Brwn; Cart; CGar; Chil; D&D; EWK; John; JWB; Mars; MAS; Mole; OGC; SbS; SMM; Sutt; T&M; Tuck; Unwi; VanH; Yate

Stanis
Suppliers: Toze

Stone
Suppliers: Dob; Toze

F1 Tokyo Cross
Suppliers: Bree; CGar; Dob; EWK; Foth; OGC; SbS; T&M; Yate
Tyfon
Suppliers: Bree; JWB; MAS
Veitch's Red Globe
Suppliers: OGC
Synonyms
De Norfolk a collet vert see Imperial Green Globe
Early White see Snowball
Goudbal see Golden Ball
Green Globe see Imperial Green Globe
Green Top Stone see Manchester Market
Milan White Top see Milan White
Model White see Stone
Norfolk Green Globe see Imperial Green Globe
Orange Jelly see Golden Ball
Sprinter see Milan Purple Top Forcing
Stubble Turnip see Typhon
Tokyo Market Sagami see Presto
Veitch's Red Globe see Purple Top White Globe

Watercress
Nasturtium officinalis
Imperial Large Leaved
Suppliers: SbS
Watercress
Suppliers: Butc; CGar; Cham; Chil; Dob; EWK; JWB; Mole; OGC; Rog; SbS; SMM; Suff; Sutt

Watermelon
Citrullus lanatus
Charleston Gray
Suppliers: CGar; EWK; JWB; Mole; OGC; SbS; SMM
Crimson Sweet
Suppliers: John
F1 Golden Crown
Suppliers: T&M
Lucky Sweet
Suppliers: Bakk

Suppliers

Bakk   **Bakker Holland**
P.O. Box 111
Spalding
Lincs
PE12 6EL
Phone   0775 711411
Latest catalogue is 1992.

Barb   **John Barber Ltd**
Old Cross Wharf
Hertford
SG14 1RB
Phone   0922 582304

Bree   **Breeders Seeds Ltd**
17 Summerwood Lane
Halsall
Ormskirk
Lancs
L39 8RQ
Phone   0704 840775
Fax   0704 841099
Specialises in bulk supplies,
but some small packets also
available. Latest catalogue is
1992.

Brwn   **D. T. Brown & Co Ltd**
Station Road
Poulton Le Fylde
Blackpool
FY6 7HX
Phone   0253 882371
Fax   0253 890923
Some bulk supplies, but also
a good range of small
packets.

Butc   **Thomas Butcher**
60 Wickham Road
Shirley
Croydon
Surrey
CR9 8AG
Phone   081 654 3720
Latest catalogue is 1992.

CGar   **Country Gardens**
69/71 Main Street
East Leake
Leics
LE12 6PF
Phone   0509 852905

Cart   **Carters Tested Seeds Ltd**
Hele Road
Torquay
Devon TQ2 7QJ
Phone   0803 616156
Fax   0803 615747

Cham   **John Chambers**
15 Westleigh Road
Barton Seagrave
Kettering
Northants
NN15 5AJ
Phone   0933 652562
Fax   0933 652576
Famous for wild flowers, but
also supply many edible
"weeds" and other unusual
pot-herbs and vegetables.
Latest catalogue is 1992.

Chil **Chiltern Seeds**
Bortree Stile
Ulverston
Cumbria
LA12 7PB
Phone   0229 581137
Fax   0229 54549
An astonishing range of
seeds, apart from vegetables.
Latest catalogue is 1992.

D&D **Dig and Delve Organics**
Fen Road
Blo' Norton
Diss
Norfolk
IP22 2JH
Phone   0379 898377

Dob **Samuel Dobie & Son Ltd**
Broomhill Way
Torquay
Devon
TQ2 7QW
Phone   0803 616888

EWK **E.W.King & Co. Ltd**
Monks Farm
Pantlings Lane
Coggeshall Road
Kelvedon
CO5 9PG
Phone   0376 570000
Bulk supplies and smaller
packets. A major wholesaler
for other seed suppliers.

Foth **Mr Fothergill's Seeds Ltd**
Gazeley Road
Kentford
Newmarket
Suffolk
CB8 7QB

Futu **Future Foods**
3 Tai Madog
Stablau
Llanrug
Gwynedd
LL5 3PH
Phone   0286 870606
A truly wonderful catalogue,
full of unusual edible plants.
We have listed only the
vegetables; Future Foods also
supply trees and shrubs,
unusual fruits, mushroom
spawns, and starter cultures
for fermented foods. Latest
catalogue is 1992.

Hen **James Henderson & Sons**
Kingholm Quay
Dumfries
DG1 4SU
Phone   0387 52234
Fax   0387 62302
A potato specialist.

JWB **J.W. Boyce Seedsmen**
Bush Pasture
Lower Carter Street
Fordham, Ely
Cambs
CB7 5JU
Phone   0638 721158
Latest catalogue is 1992.

| John | W.W. Johnson & Son Ltd | McL | Mrs M. MacLean |

John   **W.W. Johnson & Son Ltd**
London Road
Boston
Lincs
PE21 8AD
Phone   0205 365051
Fax   0205 310148
Latest catalogue is 1992.

MAS   **M.A.S.**
9 Brevel Terrace
Charlton Kings
Cheltenham
GL53 8JZ
Phone   0242 234355
Bulk only. Specialist in grass
mixtures for all purposes.
Also wildflowers and
conservation mixtures.

Mars   **S.E. Marshall & Co**
Wisbech
Cambs
PE13 2RF
Phone   0945 583407

Mart   **J.E. Martin**
4 Church Street
Market Harborough
Leics
LE16 7AA
Phone   0858 462751
A potato specialist.

McL   **Mrs M. MacLean**
Dornock Farm
Crieff
Perthshire
PH7 3QN
Phone   0764 2472
Wonderful range of potatoes,
but rather limited
availability. Please send SAE
when enquiring. Two
information leaflets
available: Fact Sheet on
Special Properties of Potato
Varieties (revised 1990, price
50p) and Growing Potatoes
for Exhibition (1987, price
30p).

Mole   **J. W. Moles & Son**
London Road
Stanway
Colchester
Essex
CO3 5PD
Phone   0206 576710
Fax   0206 575463
Bulk only.

OGC   **Chase Organics (GB) Ltd**
Coombelands House
Coombelands Lane
Addlestone
Weybridge
KT15 1HY
Phone   0932 820958
HDRA's own catalogue.

Pask   **A.R. Paske**
The South Lodge
Gazeley Road
Kentford, Newmarket
SUFFOLK
CB8 7QA
Phone   0638 750613
Supplier of seakale thongs.

Poyn   **Poyntzfield Herb Nursery**
Black Isle
By Dingwall
Ross-shire
Scotland
IV7 8LX
Phone   (038 18) 352
Specialist herb nursery, with
many unusual edible plants
beyond those listed.
Organically grown seeds and
plants. Send 3 1st class
stamps and SAE for
catalogue.

RSlu   **Royal Sluis Ltd**
P.O. Box 34
Unit 24 Marathon Place
Moss Side Estate
Leyland
PR5 3QT
Bulk only.

Rob   **W. Robinson & Sons Ltd**
Sunny Bank
Forton
Nr Preston
Lancs
PR3 0BN
Phone   0524 791210
Specialist in giant and
exhibition varieties.

Rog   **R. V. Roger Ltd**
The Nurseries
Pickering
North Yorkshire
YO18 7HG
Phone   0751 72226
Latest catalogue is 1992.

SMM   **S.M.McArd (Seeds)**
39 West Road
Pointon
Sleaford
Lincs
NG34 0NA
Bulk & small supplies.

SbS   **Seeds-By-Size**
45 Crouchfield
Hemel Hempstead
Herts
HP1 1PA
Phone   0442 251458
An amazing range of
vegetable varieties. Latest
catalogue is 1992.

Scot   **Scotston Garden Potatoes**
Scotston
Laurencekirk
Grampian
AB3 1ND
Phone   05617 447
Potato specialist. Some
doubt whether the company
is still trading.

Suff   **Suffolk Herbs Ltd**
Sawyers Farm
Little Cornard
Sudbury
Suffolk
CO10 0NY
Phone   0787 227247
Fax   0787 227258
Latest catalogue is 1992.

Sutt   **Suttons Seeds Ltd**
Hele Road
Torquay
Devon
TQ2 7QJ
Phone   0803 614455

T&M   **Thompson & Morgan (Ipswich) Ltd**
London Road
Ipswich
Suffolk
IP2 0BA
Phone   0473 688821
Fax   0473 680199

Toze   **A.L. Tozer Ltd**
Pyports
Downside Bridge Road
Cobham
SURREY
KT11 3EH
Phone   0932 862059
Fax   0932 868973
Larger quantities only.

Tuck   **Edwin Tucker and Sons Ltd**
Brewery Meadow
Stone Park, Ashburton
Newton Abbot
Devon
TQ13 7DG
Phone   0364 52403

Unwi   **Unwins Seeds Ltd**
Mail Order Department
Histon
Cambridge
CB4 4ZZ
Phone   0945 588522

VanH   **Van Hage Seed Specialists**
Great Amwell
Ware
Herts
SG12 9RP
Phone   0920 870811

Webs   **Websters Seed Potatoes**
6 Denside
Letham Grange
Arbroath
Tayside
DD11 4QL
Phone   024189 358
Potato specialist.

Yate   **Samuel Yates Ltd**
Withyfold Drive
Macclesfield
Cheshire
SK10 2BE
Phone   0625 427823
Fax   0625 422843
Bulk only.